Using and Understanding Maps

How To Read A Map

Consulting Editor

Scott E. Morris

College of Mines and Earth Resources
University of Idaho

Chelsea House Publishers
New York   Philadelphia

This Publication was designed, edited and computer generated by
Lovell Johns Limited
10 Hanborough Business Park
Long Hanborough
Witney
Oxon, England OX8 8LH

General Editor and Project Manager   Alison Dickinson
Research and Text   Gill Lloyd

The contents of this volume are based on the latest data available at the
time of publication.

Map credit: *Antarctica source map prepared at 1:20,000 by the British
Antarctic Survey Mapping and Geographic Information Centre, 1990*

Cover credit: *Tom Stewart/The Stock Market*

Printed in Mexico

3 5 7 9 8 6 4

Library of Congress Cataloging in Publication Data

How To Read A Map /editorial consultant, Scott Morris:
        p. cm.—(Using and understanding maps)
        Includes bibliographical references and index.
        Summary: Describes how to use and understand maps and apply
        them in the study of geography, cartography, and social studies.
        ISBN 0-7910-1812-1. — ISBN 0-7910-1825-3 (pbk.)
        1. Maps—Juvenile literature. [1. Maps.
        I. Chelsea House Publishers.   II Series.
        GA105.6.S76 1993
        912 — dc20   92-22824
                                                    CIP
                                                    AC

Introduction

We inhabit a fascinating and mysterious planet where the earth's physical features, life-forms, and the diversity of human culture conspire to produce a breathtaking environment. We don't have to travel very far to see and experience the wealth of this diverse planet; in fact, we don't have to travel at all. Everywhere images of the world are abundantly available in books, newspapers, magazines, movies, television, and the arts. We could say that *everywhere* one looks, our world is a brilliant moving tapestry of shapes, colors, and textures, and our experience of its many messages — whether in our travels or simply by gazing out into our own backyards — is what we call reality.

Geography is the study of a portion of that reality. More so, it is the study of how the physical and biological components (rocks, animals, plants, and people) of our planet are distributed and how they are interconnected. Geographers seek to describe and to explain the physical patterns that have evolved on the earth and also to discover the significance in the ways they have evolved. To do this, geographers rely on maps.

Maps can be powerful images. They convey selective information about vast areas of an overwhelmingly cluttered world. The cartographer, or mapmaker, must carefully choose the theme of a map, that is, what it will show, knowing that a good map will convey the essence of information while at the same time making the information easy to comprehend.

This volume and its companions in UNDERSTANDING AND USING MAPS are about the planet we call earth and the maps we use to find our way along its peaks and valleys. Each volume displays map images that reveal how the world is arranged according to a specific theme such as population, industries or the endangered world. The maps in each volume are accompanied by an interesting collection of facts — some are rather obvious, others are oddities. Yet all are meant to be informative.

Along with a wealth of facts, there are explanations of the various attributes and phenomena depicted by the maps. This information is provided to better understand the significance of the maps as well as to demonstrate how the many themes relate.

Names for places are essential to geographers. To study the world without devising names for places would be extremely difficult. But geographers also know that names are in no way permanent; place names change as people change. The recent reunification of Germany and the breakup of what was the Soviet Union — events that seem colossal from the perspective of socioeconomics — to geographers are simply events that require the drawing or erasing of one or a few boundaries and the renaming of one or several land masses. The geographer is constantly reminded that the world is in flux; a map is always in danger of being rendered obsolete by a turn in current events.

Because the world is dynamic, it continues to captivate the mind and stimulate the imagination. USING AND UNDERSTANDING MAPS presents the world as it is today, with the reservation that any dramatic rearrangement of land and people is likely, indeed inevitable, thus requiring the making of a new map. In this way maps are themselves a part of the evolutionary process.

Scott E. Morris

How to Read a Map

Over the past 500 years or so, most people have come to realize that the world is a very big place. If you started out walking around the full circumference of the earth and walked at a comfortable pace, 8 hours a day, 5 days a week, 50 weeks a year, you would not return to where you began for over 6 years! And still, you would have seen only a small fraction of the earth's surface. In such a big place, maps are essential. They are the way we arrange this big world so that we can comprehend and study it.

We have grown up in the information age and know more about our planet that ever before. Much of this information "belongs" to places we have visited, read about, or viewed in pictures and movies. By attaching information to a place, we make a map.

We carry around in our minds maps of our world. Whenever you go somewhere, you must have a map in your own mind as to how to get there. You know where your school is, where your friends live, where the ice cream store is located, and countless other pieces of geographic information.

The modern science of cartography is concerned with the organization and display of this spatial information. Like many sciences, cartography developed from a practical need. Trade between countries, whether by land routes or by sea, required maps. As the distances people traveled increased, new maps were drawn. As techniques for measuring distances and locations improved, old maps were revised in more accurate form. The process continues even today as human civilization adds new "features" to the earth's surface. Political boundaries are being redrawn in Europe, Asia, and Africa. New landscape is being made by volcanic eruptions in Iceland, Hawaii, Central America, and other places. Maps are even being drawn of places we have never been, like the planets Mars, Venus, and Jupiter.

Mapmaking is not a simple endeavor. The goal is always to accurately reproduce the geographic arrangement of features at some different, more convenient size. Obviously, a map of your city at its true scale would be useless. It would cover the city when you unfolded it! Most maps are drawn at a smaller scale; a small distance on the map represents a large distance on the ground. Because of this scale reduction, not all features can be shown. The cartographer, then, is faced with the decision about what to include on a map. If the map becomes too cluttered, it will be very difficult to use. Many maps are thematic. They show a specific attribute in great detail, often sacrificing other nonessential information.

There are other cartographic problems that are not immediately obvious. Most maps are of the earth's surface, which is spherical. Location is a problem; a sphere has no top, bottom, or edges. Our location system of latitude and longitude literally comes from outer space. In cartographic terms, the sphere is undevelopable, which means that it cannot be unrolled or unfolded to lie flat. As such, no map of a spherical surface can accurately portray distance, area, and shape at the same time. So again, cartographers must choose appropriate methods — called projections — to suit the most important purpose of the map.

This volume is about the many different kinds of maps, how they are made, and how they can be used. Learning about cartography is essential to understanding our world. If a picture is worth a thousand words, a good map may be worth a million.

Scott E. Morris

legend lists and explains the symbols and colors sed on the map. It is called a legend because it ells the story of a map. It is important to read the map legend to find out exactly what the symbols mean because some symbols do not look like what they represent. For example, a dot stands for a town.

very map in this atlas has a legend on it.

This legend lists and explains the colors and symbols used on the map on that page only. The legend on the left, below, shows examples of the colors used on the maps in all the atlases in this series. Below this is a list of all symbols used on the maps in all the atlases in this series.

The legend on the right, below, is an example of a legend used in the physical atlas.

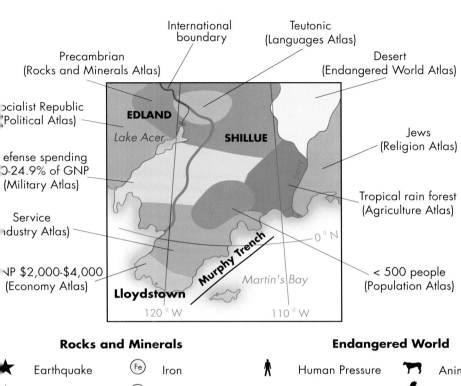

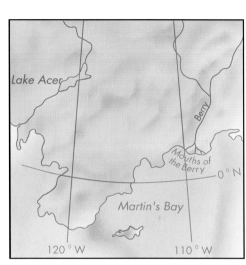

Rocks and Minerals

★ Earthquake	(Fe) Iron	
▲ Volcano	(Pb) Lead	
Coal	(Mn) Manganese	
Natural gas	(Pt) Platinum	
Oil	(Ag) Silver	
Diamonds	(S) Sulfur	
Uranium	(Sn) Tin	
Bauxite	(Ti) Titanium	
Copper	(Zn) Zinc	
Gold		

Languages

African Tribal Languages	Indian
★ Creole	◇ Caucasian
Aborigine	■ Dravidian
Basque	
✝ Swahili	● Kurdish

Religion

Important religious place

Endangered World

🧍 Human Pressure	🐃 Animals at Risk
🐄 Animal Pressure	🦅 Birds at Risk
💧 Acid Rain	

Industry

Oil Refining	Food and Drink
Hydroelectric Power	Heavy Industry
Nuclear Power	Chemicals
Ships	Textiles
Aircraft	Metals
Trains	Light Industry
Cars	Plastics

Economy

1 Bundle = $1 Billion GNP	1 Coin = $10 Billion GNP
1 Coin = $500 Million GNP	World's Largest Stock Exchanges

Physical

▲ Mountain Peak	Canal

Agriculture and Vegetation

Wheat	Grapes	
Barley	Fruit	
Maize	Timber	
Rice	Tobacco	
Oats	Coconuts	
Cocoa	Rubber	
Cotton	Cattle	
Silk	Sheep	
Sugar	Olives	
Coffee	Soybeans	
Tea	Potatoes	
Palm Oil		

Military

🪖 Number of armed forces per 1,000 population	Member of NATO

Political

Number of Political Parties	★ Capital City

This page is a physical map of the world. It indicates where the major physical features — such as mountain ranges, plains, deserts, lakes, and rivers — are in the world. As the world is very large, the map has to be drawn at a very small scale in order to fit onto a page. This map is drawn at a scale so that 1 inch on the map, at the equator, equals 1,840 miles on the ground.

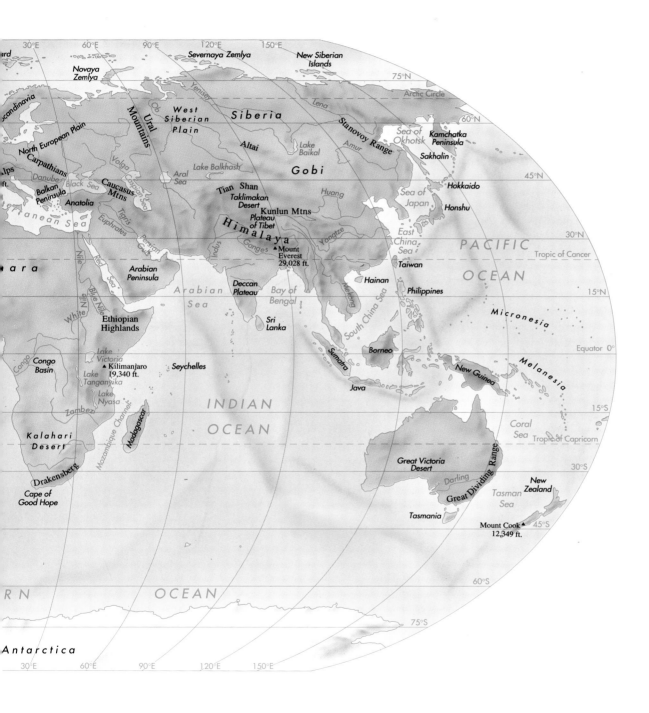

30°E 60°E 90°E 120°E 150°E

Severnaya Zemlya

New Siberian
Islands

Novaya
Zemlya

75°N

Arctic Circle

andinavia

West
Siberian
Plain

Ural Mountains

Siberia

Stanovoy Range

60°N

Sea of
Okhotsk

Kamchatka
Peninsula

North European Plain

Altai

Lake
Baikal

Amur

Sakhalin

Volga

Carpathians

Danube

Caspian Sea

Lake Balkhash

Gobi

45°N

Black Sea

Aral
Sea

Hokkaido

Alps

ft.

Balkan
Peninsula

Caucasus
Mtns

Tian Shan
Taklimakan
Desert

Huang

Sea of
Japan

Honshu

Anatolia

Euphrates

Tigris

Kunlun Mtns
Plateau
of Tibet

Himalaya

Yangtze

East
China
Sea

30°N

terranean Sea

Nile

Red Sea

Persian Gulf

Indus

Ganges

▲ Mount
Everest
29,028 ft.

PACIFIC

Tropic of Cancer

ara

Arabian
Peninsula

Arabian
Sea

Deccan
Plateau

Bay of
Bengal

Taiwan

OCEAN

15°N

Mekong

Hainan

Philippines

Blue Nile

Ethiopian
Highlands

Sri
Lanka

South China Sea

Micronesia

White

Lake
Victoria

Kilimanjaro
19,340 ft.

Seychelles

Sumatra

Borneo

Equator 0°

Congo

Congo
Basin

Lake
Tanganyika

Java

New Guinea

Melanesia

Lake
Nyasa

Zambezi

INDIAN

15°S

Kalahari
Desert

Mozambique Channel

Madagascar

OCEAN

Coral
Sea

Tropic of Capricorn

Drakensberg

Great Victoria
Desert

Great Dividing Range

New
Zealand

30°S

Cape of
Good Hope

Darling

Tasman
Sea

Tasmania

Mount Cook ▲
12,349 ft.

45°S

60°S

RN

OCEAN

75°S

Antarctica

30°E 60°E 90°E 120°E 150°E

World Key Map

Africa, Northern 10-11

Algeria
Benin
Burkina Faso
Cameroon
Cape Verde
Central African Republic
Chad
Djibouti
Egypt
Ethiopia
Gambia
Ghana
Guinea
Guinea-Bissau
Ivory Coast
Liberia
Libya
Mali
Mauritania
Morocco
Niger
Nigeria
Senegal
Sierra Leone
Somalia
Sudan
Togo
Tunisia
Western Sahara

Africa, Southern 12-13

Angola
Botswana
Burundi
Comoros
Congo
Equatorial Guinea
Gabon
Kenya
Lesotho
Madagascar
Malawi
Mauritius
Mozambique
Namibia
Rwanda
São Tomé & Príncipe
Seychelles
South Africa
Swaziland
Tanzania
Uganda
Zaire
Zambia
Zimbabwe

America, Central 14-15

Antigua & Barbuda
Bahamas
Barbados
Belize
Costa Rica
Cuba
Dominica
Dominican Republic
El Salvador
Grenada
Guatemala
Haiti
Honduras
Jamaica
Mexico
Nicaragua
Panama
St Kitts - Nevis
St Lucia
St Vincent
Trinidad & Tobago

Canada
26-27

United States
of America
40-41

Central
America
14-15

Oceania
38-39

South America
16-17

Canada 26-27

Canada

Commonwealth of Independent States 28-29

Armenia
Azerbaijan
Estonia
Georgia
Kazakhstan
Kirghizstan
Latvia
Lithuania
Moldova
Russian Federation
Tajikistan
Turkmenistan
Ukraine
Uzbekhistan

Europe 30-31

Albania
Bosnia & Herzegovina
Bulgaria
Croatia
Czechoslovakia
Finland
Greece
Hungary
Iceland
Norway
Poland
Romania
Slovenia
Sweden
Yugoslavia

Europe, Western 32-33

Andorra
Austria
Belgium
Denmark
France
Germany
Ireland
Italy
Liechtenstein
Luxembourg
Malta
Monaco
Netherlands
Portugal
San Marino
Spain
Switzerland
United Kingdom
Vatican City

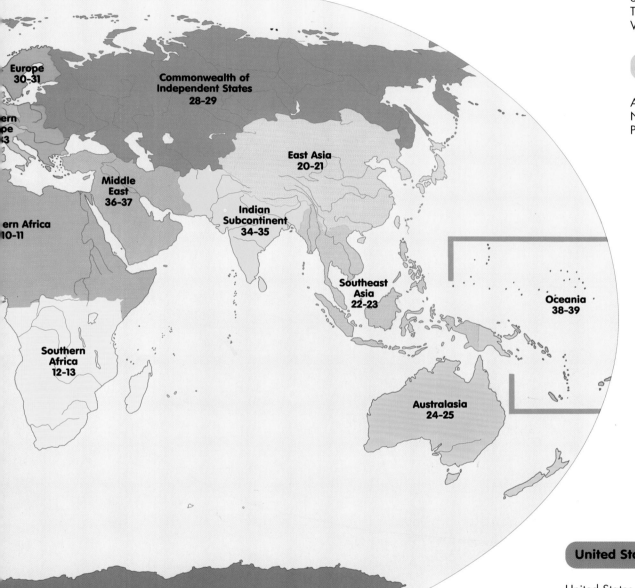

Being able to locate our exact position on earth has always been a very important skill. The system for finding out where you are is based on a series of grid lines known as latitude and longitude.

Latitude and Longitude

The world is shaped like a round ball, so it can be depicted quite accurately as a globe and divided up into sections using imaginary lines that enable anyone on land, sea, or in the air to work out their exact position.

Lines of latitude run in an east-to-west direction around the earth. Midway around the earth lies the most important line of latitude, called the equator and numbered 0°. North of the equator, the number on each line of latitude increases until you reach the pole, numbered 90° N. The numbers increase as you move southward from the equator, until you reach the South Pole, which is 90° S.

Latitude gives you a position north or south of the equator, and as the lines run parallel to one another they are known as parallels. They are measured in degrees, and each degree can be further subdivided into 60 minutes.

Lines of longitude run from the North Pole to the South Pole and are known as meridians. The most important is the prime meridian (0°), which runs through Greenwich in England. Longitude is measured from the prime meridian; those lines to the west are labelled W and those to the east E. There are 360 degrees of longitude, so the lines meet at the opposite side of the globe at 180°. 180° W and 180° E are therefore the same line.

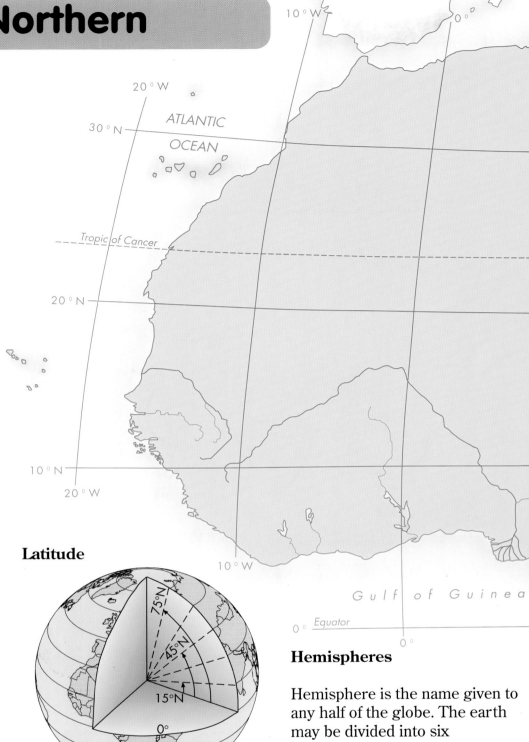

Latitude

Parallels of latitude

Longitude

Meridians of longitude

Hemispheres

Hemisphere is the name given to any half of the globe. The earth may be divided into six hemispheres. The Eastern Hemisphere, or Old World, contains the continents of Europe, Asia, Africa, and Australia. The New World is in the Western Hemisphere and consists of North and South America. Geographers usually make the boundary between the Eastern and Western Hemispheres along the meridians 20° W and 160° E. The equator also acts as a boundary between hemispheres. Anything in the north is in the Northern Hemisphere, everything south of the equator in the Southern Hemisphere.

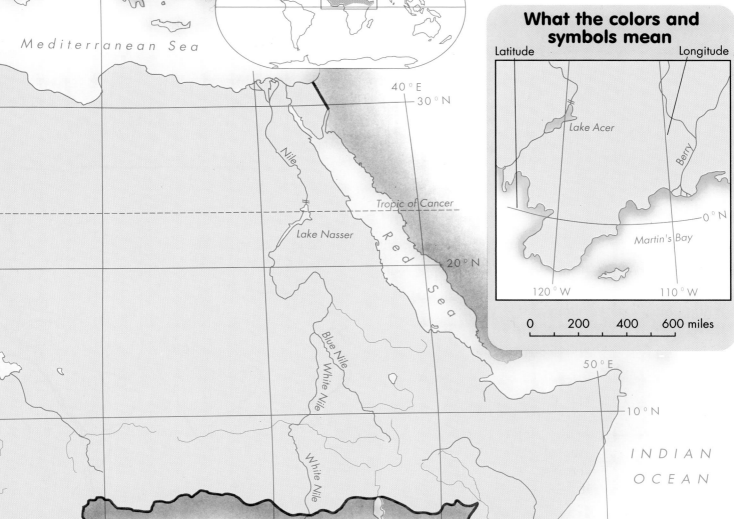

20° E

Mediterranean Sea

40° E
30° N

Nile

Tropic of Cancer

Lake Nasser

Red Sea

20° N

Blue Nile

White Nile

50° E

10° N

White Nile

INDIAN
OCEAN

Equator
0°

E

20° E

30° E

40° E

50° E

What the colors and symbols mean

Latitude   Longitude

Lake Acer

Berry

0° N

Martin's Bay

120° W   110° W

0   200   400   600 miles

The world is sometimes divided up into land and water hemispheres. The land hemisphere is centered around London or Paris and is the half of the globe, mainly north of the equator, that contains about six-sevenths of the land surface. The water hemisphere is the half of the globe that consists mainly of ocean, lying south of the equator and usually centered near New Zealand.

Northern Hemisphere

Land Hemisphere

Southern Hemisphere

Western Hemisphere

Eastern Hemisphere

Water Hemisphere

Africa, Southern

Directions on the earth are really entirely based on accepted practices, because logically a spherical object has no edges, no beginning, and no end. However, without an accepted system there would be no means of explaining, defining, or measuring where you are in the world.

Direction

The system of latitude and longitude defines anything north-south as along a meridian and anything east-west as along a parallel. The arrangement of the latitude and longitude lines form a graticule where these two directions are everywhere perpendicular, except at the poles. The directions given by the graticule are called geographic, or true, directions.

Centuries ago it became established practice to arrange maps with north at the top. We now speak of "up north" and "down south" and think of Australia as "down under." Since there is really no up or down on a sphere, there is no reason why maps or globes could not be oriented the other way up; however, this has become the convention.

 Did You Know

★ The reason why it is hotter at the equator than at the poles is because of the angle of the rays of the sun. The sun's rays shine down directly overhead at midday at the equator. Near the poles, however, the sun rarely climbs far above the horizon; the rays reach the ground at an angle and are spread out over the surface.

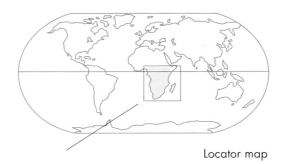

Locator map

The Tropics

The Tropic of Cancer lies on the parallel of latitude at $23\frac{1}{2}°$ N, and it marks the most northerly position at which the sun appears directly overhead at noon. The sun shines vertically over the Tropic of Cancer on the summer solstice. The Tropic of Capricorn lies on the parallel of latitude at $23\frac{1}{2}°$ S and marks the extreme southern position at which the sun's rays appear directly overhead at noon. This occurs on the winter solstice. In the Southern Hemisphere the summer and winter solstice are reversed.

The Tropics and the equator have been recognized since ancient times. Early Mediterranean astronomers discovered that the sun seemed to follow a path that changed with the seasons of the year. In winter, it crossed the southern part of the sky, and shadows were long. Then the sun moved northward, and shadows grew shorter. On one summer day at noon, shadows were shortest of all, after which they became longer again. This seemed to mean that the path of the sun turned, and the turning place was called a tropic, from the Greek word for "turning."

Understanding of the turning points of the sun's path was very useful for early mapmakers. It enabled them to established a line, or parallel, through the points, which gave a fixed reference on the earth's surface. This enabled distances north and south to be measured.

Location Maps

On each map page of this book, yo will see that there is a small location map that indicates the par of the world that has been highlighted on that page. If you turn to the page on Australia, the location map has been drawn from a different perspective than the on used on this page. These are drawn to help in getting a clear orientatio of the area on a world map.

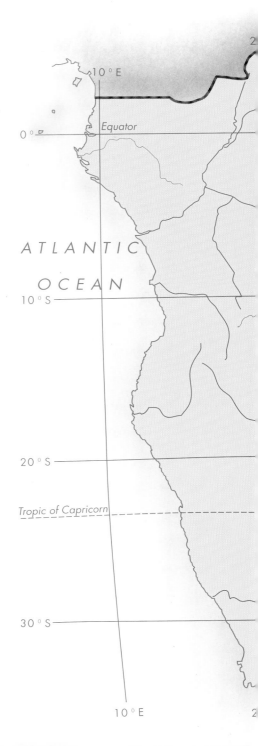

eat Circles

reat circle is a circle on the rface of the earth that, if it were slice through the center of the rth, would divide it into two nispheres. The equator is a eat circle, as are two opposite ridians. The shortest distance ween any two points on the rface of the earth can be found the arc of the great circle that sses through both points. Ships sea and aircraft on long-distance rneys often follow great circle tes.

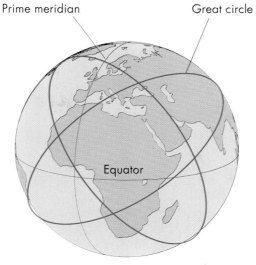

Prime meridian Great circle

Equator

As great circles are shortcuts, they are good routes for ships and aircraft to follow on long-distance journeys.

What the colors and symbols mean

Latitude Longitude

Lake Acer

Berry

0° N

Martin's Bay

120° W 110° W

0 200 400 600 miles

30° E 40° E 50° E

Equator 0°

INDIAN

OCEAN

Lake Victoria

Lake Tanganyika

Lake Nyasa

10° S

Mozambique Channel

Madagascar

20° S

Tropic of Capricorn

30° S

30° E 40° E 50° E

The length of a degree of latitude

Degrees of latitude are very nearly all the same. One degree of latitude is about 60 nautical miles or 69 land miles.
The earth is not a perfect sphere so a degree of latitude varies from 59.7 nautical miles at the equator to 60.3 nautical miles near the poles.

The length of a degree of longitude

The distance between meridians of longitude on the equator is about 69 miles. However, as the lines get closer to the North and South Poles, the number of miles in a degree of longitude decreases.

! Amazing – But True

★ A map using the gnomonic projection shows a great circle route as a straight line; any other projection shows the route as a curved line.

The simplest way of determining directions is with a compass, which is basically a magnetized needle placed on a pivot so it can move freely. The needle points in the direction of the earth's magnetic North Pole. Since every map is printed with north at the top, to read a map correctly in an unknown country, a compass must be used.

Who discovered the compass?

It is believed that the Chinese invented the compass over a thousand years ago. Early compasses were made of simple pieces of magnetic iron, usually floating in straw or cork in a bowl of water. European navigators knew how to use the compass by 1187, but there is no historical record of who brought it to Europe. By the 1300s the compass card was marked off into 32 points of direction, and in the following years navigators began to understand about the deviation or variation of compasses in different parts of the world.

Amazing – But True

★ Six hundred years ago there were many people who thought that the compass was invented by the devil. They were afraid of the needles that always swung around to point north.

★ The Vikings needed something to help them find out which direction they were traveling in because sailing in the foggy North Atlantic they could seldom see the sun or stars. In bad weather they often waited for birds to fly overhead, then followed them to shore.

Points of the compass

There are four main points of the compass, north, east, south, and west. These are known as the cardinal points. Between these lie the intercardinal points, which are northeast, southeast, southwest, and northwest. Modern compasses are marked clockwise with the 360 degrees of a circle.

Gyrocompass

When iron and steel ships were built in the 1800s, making an accurate compass became very difficult, as the readings were affected by the ships. As a result the gyrocompass was invented. It is not affected by magnetism and points to true north. Another advantage is that it is mounted in such a way that it always stays level.

Compass Deviation

When a magnetic compass is placed near a metal object that contains iron, it is attracted to that object. The angle that is formed between the north magnetic pole and the direction in which the compass points is known as deviation.

A pocket compass

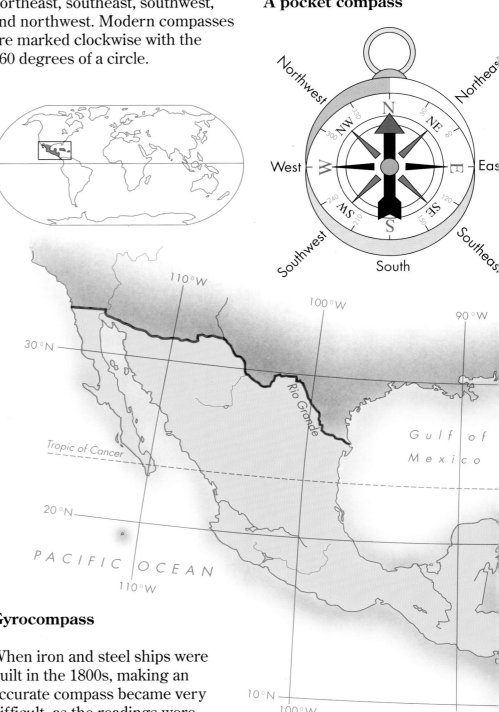

A ship's gyrocompass maintaining due north.

Compass Variation

The earth behaves as though there [is] a large magnet at its center and attracts the small magnet used in a compass needle. The axis of the earth's magnet is not the same line that joins the North and South poles. Therefore a compass needle does not point to the true North pole. The difference between the true North Pole and the magnetic North is called the magnetic declination. This is often marked on maps and has to be taken into account by those navigating at sea or in the air.

Examples of north points

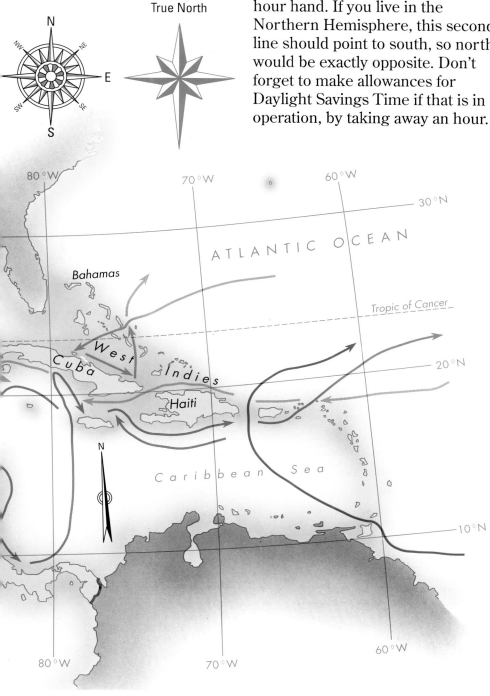

True North

How to set your map

Place your compass on your map, and wait for the needle to point to the north. Keeping the compass steady, move the map round until the top of the map points to the north as shown by the compass needle.

If you don't have a compass, you can still set your map using a wristwatch. Point the hour hand toward the sun, or toward where you know the sun would be if you could see it. Now visualize a line joining the center of the watch face to the figure 12. Imagine a line halfway between this line and the hour hand. If you live in the Northern Hemisphere, this second line should point to south, so north would be exactly opposite. Don't forget to make allowances for Daylight Savings Time if that is in operation, by taking away an hour.

Using a wristwatch to set a map

Christopher Columbus discovers the Caribbean

Christopher Columbus sailed westward in search of a quicker sea route to India, but he did not realize that Mexico lay between him and the Indies. On his first voyage he landed on one of the islands of the Bahamas on October 12, 1492, believing it to be an island in Asia. On his second voyage to the Caribbean, Columbus landed on Cuba and Haiti, believing the former island to be Japan. Columbus made two more further voyages to the New World, and he was so sure that the Caribbean islands were near the mainland of India that he named them the West Indies. The four voyages have been marked on the map.

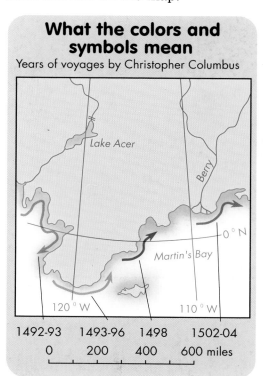

What the colors and symbols mean
Years of voyages by Christopher Columbus

1492-93	1493-96	1498	1502-04

0	200	400	600 miles

The earth is an enormous sphere that spins on its axis. Its surface consists of water and land. Water, mainly the great oceans, covers 70 percent of the surface of the earth and separates huge land masses called continents. South America is one of the seven continents of the world.

How can something as big and round as the earth be mapped?

The area of the world's surface is about 196,000,000 square miles. Water covers about 139,692,000 square miles.

Because the earth is a sphere it is impossible to represent it accurately, except on a globe. Any drawing of the world on a flat surface must have some inaccuracies and distortion.

Map Projections

A map projection is the systematic drawing of the lines of latitude and longitude from the globe onto a flat sheet of paper. The network of imaginary lines, called the graticule, forms the basis upon which an accurate image can be drawn. Some of the special qualities that are important to mapmakers are: Correct representation: Showing the areas or sizes of different regions in correct proportion to one another. True shape: Showing the correct shape of an area. Accurate directions: Showing angles and directions from any point correctly. A mapmaker can draw many separate maps to answer different questions, but it is difficult to allow for all these qualities on any one map. The choice of map projection is based upon the properties the cartographer wishes the map to possess, the scale or size of the map, and the size of the area that is being drawn.

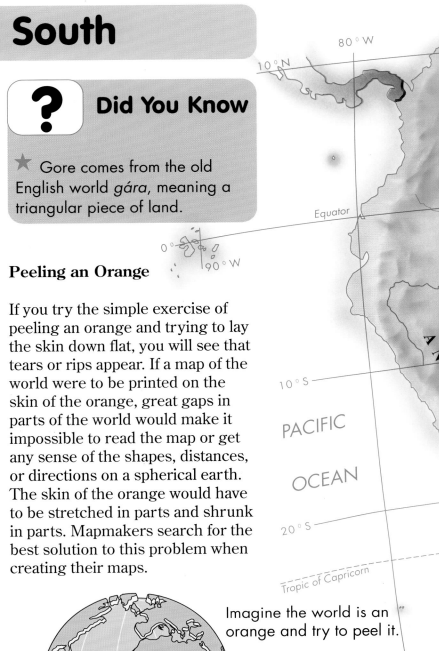

? Did You Know

⭐ Gore comes from the old English world *gára*, meaning a triangular piece of land.

Peeling an Orange

If you try the simple exercise of peeling an orange and trying to lay the skin down flat, you will see that tears or rips appear. If a map of the world were to be printed on the skin of the orange, great gaps in parts of the world would make it impossible to read the map or get any sense of the shapes, distances, or directions on a spherical earth. The skin of the orange would have to be stretched in parts and shrunk in parts. Mapmakers search for the best solution to this problem when creating their maps.

Imagine the world is an orange and try to peel it.

The strips, or gores, make this map difficult to use because gaps are left in the land and sea.

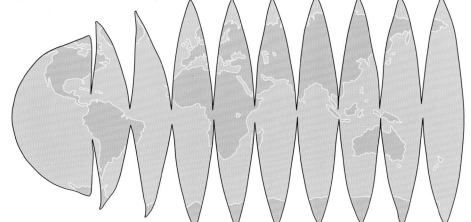

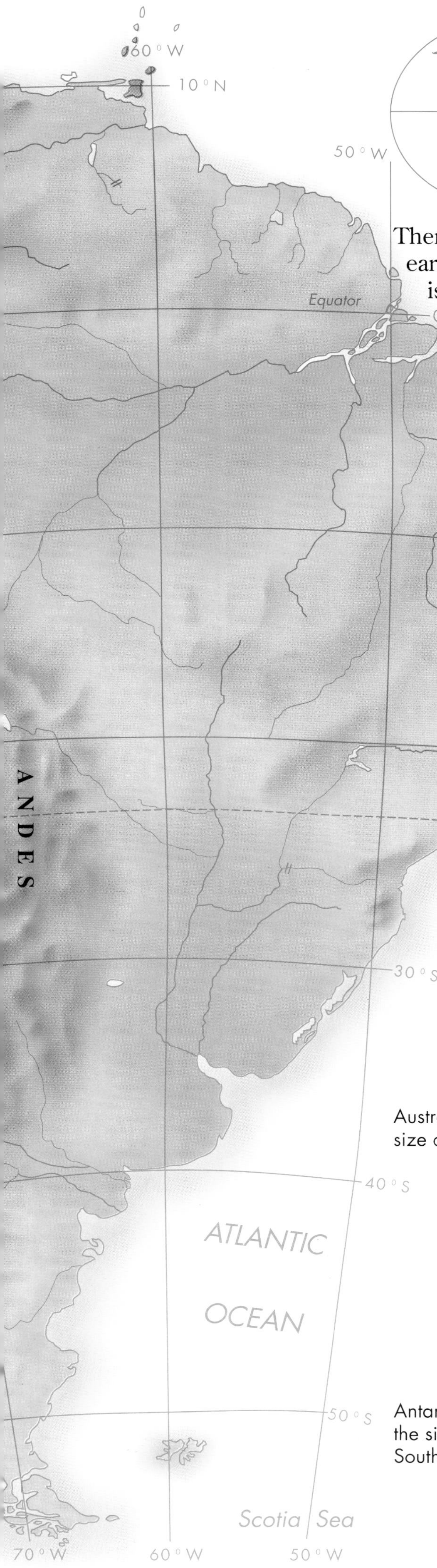

60° W

10° N

50° W

Equator

0°

40° W

10° S

20° S
40° W

30° S

40° S

ATLANTIC

OCEAN

50° S

Scotia Sea

70° W   60° W   50° W

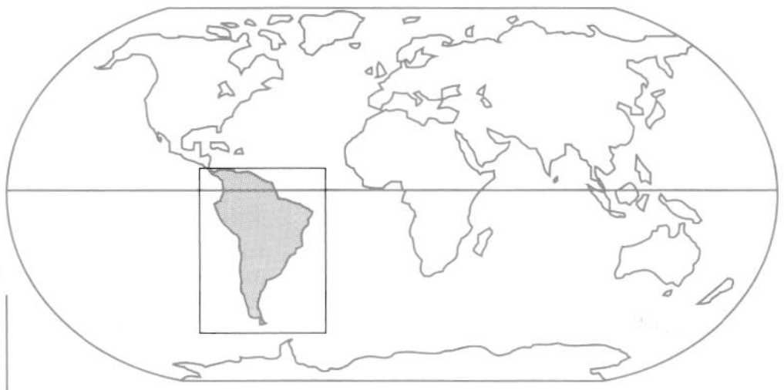

A N D E S

There are seven continents on the earth's surface. The largest continent is Asia (17,005,000 square miles) and the smallest is Australasia (2,968,000 square miles.)

North America is 1.4 times bigger than South America

Africa is 1.75 times bigger than South America

Asia is 2.5 times bigger than South America

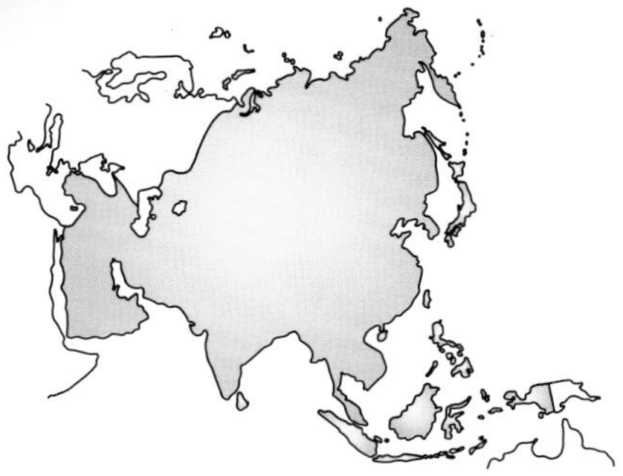

Europe is 0.6 the size of South America

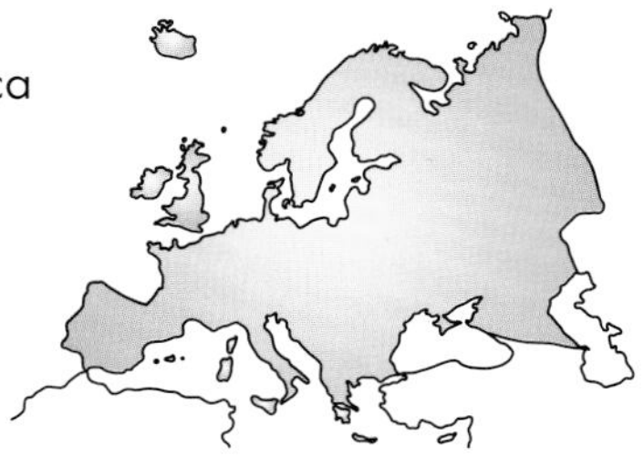

Australasia is 0.4 the size of South America

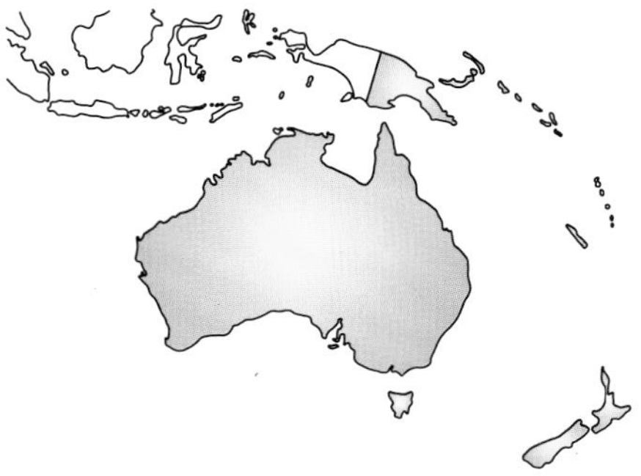

Antarctica is 0.8 times the size of South America

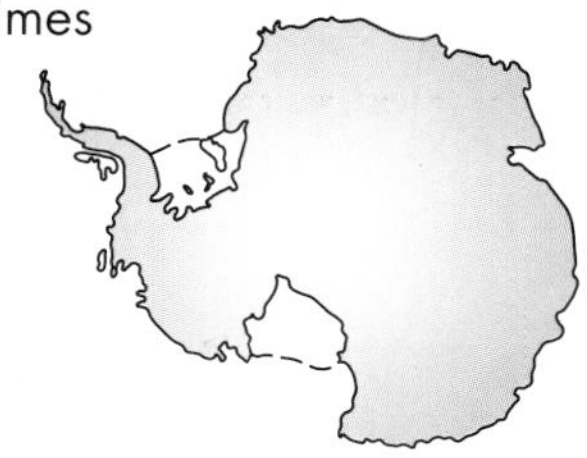

What the colors and symbols mean

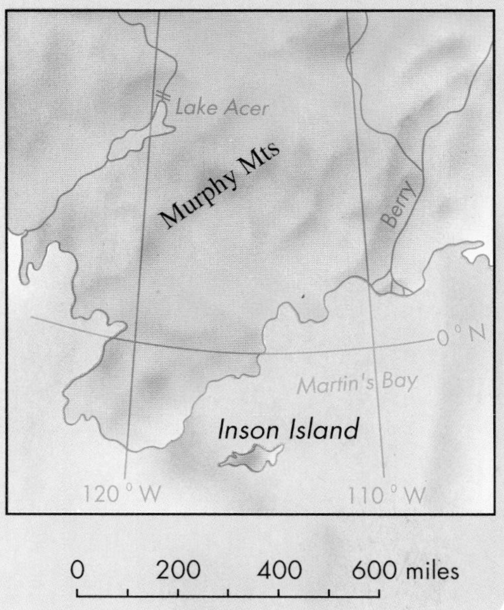

Lake Acer

Murphy Mts

Berry

0° N

Martin's Bay

Inson Island

120° W   110° W

0   200   400   600 miles

Many maps are in theory projected onto a cylinder, a cone, or a plane. There are many different forms of projection derived from these major groups. On this page we see an example of an azimuthal projection, which is ideal for showing the polar regions. Compare it with the small locator map at the top of the page, which is based on a cylindrical projection on which the polar region appears as a thin line, and you will understand the importance of finding the most suitable projection for different regions.

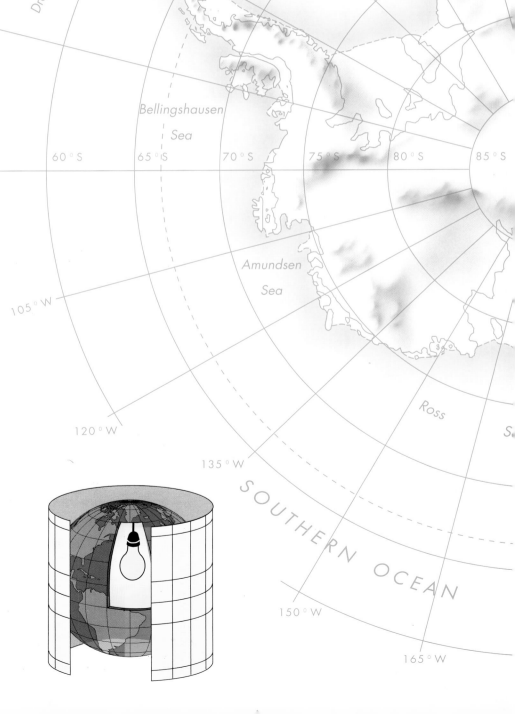

Cylindrical Projections

To understand the difference between the three main types of projections, visualize a globe with a graticule marked on it and a light within the globe projecting the lines onto a sheet of paper.
In the case of a cylindrical projection, the paper would be wrapped around the globe in a cylinder. The resulting map is accurate along the one or two lines where the paper touches the globe, but as you move away from the center near the equator toward the poles, it becomes increasingly distorted. The lines of longitude meet at the poles on the globe, and on this projection meridians are equally spaced vertical lines. Cylindrical projections basically show the globe as a rectangular shape and so seriously stretch and distort areas near the poles.

Azimuthal Projections

These can be imagined by touching an illuminated globe with a flat sheet of paper. Meridians radiate out as straight lines; parallels appear as concentric circles. The resulting map is free of distortion at the point it touches, but distortion of shape and scale increases as you move away from that point.

The map on this page demonstrates how useful this projection is for mapping compact areas such as the poles. The point from which the projection radiates can, of course, be anywhere on the globe.

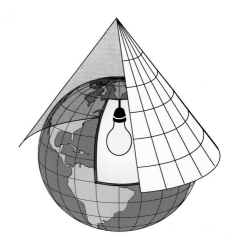

Conic Projections

Conic projections can be imagined by placing a cone of paper over a lighted globe. The map that results is free of distortion along the one or two lines of latitude where the paper touches the globe. Parallels are concentric circles; meridians are straight lines that converge at either pole. The distortion of scale increases with the distance from the parallel where the cone touches the globe. These projections work very well for countries that have large east-west dimensions and are in middle latitudes, such as the United States.

? **Did You Know**

★ One of the most famous cylindrical projections was that of Gerardus Mercator. He corrected some of the distortion by increasing the scale along the parallels, but areas away from the equator are still very inaccurate.

The most familiar kinds of maps show a variety of geographic features, including land features, water, political boundaries, cities, towns, and roads. However, there are a group of maps that are quite different, known as thematic maps. They show the distribution of a particular feature such as population, rainfall, or a natural resource.

Thematic Maps

In thematic mapping the object is to communicate information about the overall nature of a subject. Thematic maps are about patterns or distributions and express quantities or percentages by means of symbols or colors. The idea is to portray information in a visual way.

Population maps are good examples of thematic maps.

For example, tiny dots, each representing 20,000 people, could be carefully placed on a map. At a glance, it would be obvious where the population was most dense. Alternatively, color could be used to show different levels of population density.

Some thematic maps show different quantities by using lines that pass through points of equal value. An isopleth is the name given to a line on a map joining places that have equal values of some element.

Some familiar isopleths include isobars, which join places that have the same barometric pressure; isohyets, which join places that have equal rainfall over periods; isobaths, which join places that have equal depth; and isotherms, which join places of equal temperature at a particular time.

Make Your Own Thematic Map

Make a thematic map showing life expectancy by using the statistics from the Population volume in this series. The life expectancy figures from this volume are shown in graphic form. To help you, the actual figures in years have been given with the men and you can use these to create your own thematic map.

1. Trace the coastline and international boundaries from the map of East Asia on this page.

2. Color each country, using the key as a guide. The life expectancy figures for each country in East Asia fit into one of the colored bands in the key.

3. Now you have created your own thematic map showing the life expectancy for the countries in East Asia.

Life Expectancy

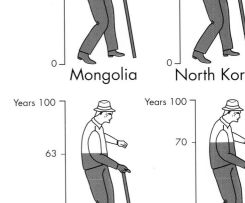

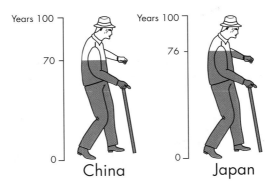

China — 70
Japan — 76
Mongolia — 62
North Kor[ea] — 63
South Korea — 63
Taiwa[n] — 70

Choosing Colors

Before maps were printed, color and pattern were drawn or painted onto manuscript maps by hand. After the 15th century, when printing of maps was more common, color was still applied by hand to each sheet, and map tinting became a specialized trade.

Cartographers have now used color for so long that certain conventions have developed, such as blue for water, black for human-made features, and green for vegetation.

In addition, certain colors have associations for people, such as red for warmth and blue for cold. These must be taken into consideration when choosing colors for a map.

(map labels:)

50°N
140°E
130°E
120°E
NORTH KOREA
Sea of Japan
JAPAN
40°N
Seoul
SOUTH KOREA
Yellow Sea
30°N
Yellow
Huang
East China Sea
PACIFIC OCEAN
Yangtze
Tropic of Cancer
20°N
140°E
TAIWAN
130°E
MACAO HONG KONG
South China Sea
110°E
120°E

ife Expectancy in Years

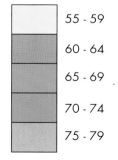

	55 - 59
	60 - 64
	65 - 69
	70 - 74
	75 - 79

? Did You Know

★ In 1855, John Snow, an English physician, gave a dramatic demonstration of the value of thematic mapping. He plotted a dot on a map of London for each person who had died of cholera that year. A mass of dots clustered around a single water pump on Broad Street gave doctors the clue to the source of the epidemic.

ompare the way in which the formation is shown on the map ou have drawn with how it is nown on the men on the left. Both ve the same information, using fferent techniques.

What the colors and symbols mean

Number of people per square mile

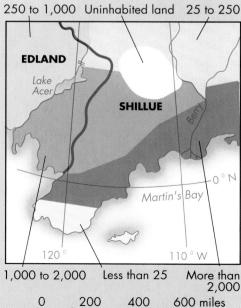

250 to 1,000   Uninhabited land   25 to 250

EDLAND
Lake Acer
SHILLUE
Berry
0°N
Martin's Bay
120°
110°W

1,000 to 2,000   Less than 25   More than 2,000

0   200   400   600 miles

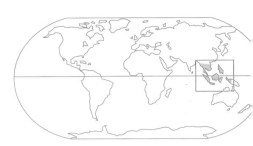

A symbol is a sign that stands for something else. In some senses a map is a symbol because it represents what occurs on the ground in a coded form. The legend is the means of decoding the symbols that appear on a map. It explains what the symbols and colors on a map represent.

Map Symbols

All sorts of features are represented on a map by symbols. They are not usually drawn to scale and may be quite exaggerated.

A road that is 20 feet wide may be shown on a map that at a true scale would represent a road 100 feet wide. Its width was exaggerated to make it visible on the map, but its length is likely to be drawn to scale.

Map symbols may be points, lines, or areas.

Point Symbols

A large number of different features are represented by point symbols, from dots used to indicate cities to the most intricate of symbolic representations. When a large number of point symbols are used on a map it is important to be able to differentiate between them with ease, and so their design is carefully planned. The main variation between symbols is in their basic form, which allows for the following:

Variations in basic shape — it is easy to see differences between such basic shapes as squares, circles, triangles, and rectangles, even when they appear very small. But this only gives a small number of basic symbols.

Picture representations such as those that appear in the legend on this page give a greater variety of symbols. Other clever ways in which symbols can be used to give additional information include:

Interruption of basic shape — for example, if a building is shown as a rectangle, an unoccupied building could be shown as a rectangle with a dotted line.

Addition to basic shape — this is one of the most productive means of creating classes of symbols. Additional lines can be added to give some meaning. For example, if a circle represents a building, additional lines can transform the symbol into a windmill, a church, or a lighthouse.

Including something within the shape — for example, on these pages the inclusion of the chemical sign for a mineral within a circle gives many possible variations.

Changes in size or color can be used to indicate relative importance.

Examples of Point Symbols

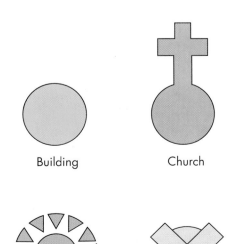

Building Church

Lighthouse Windmill

Amazing – But True

★ Tactual maps have raised symbols that blind people can read by touch.

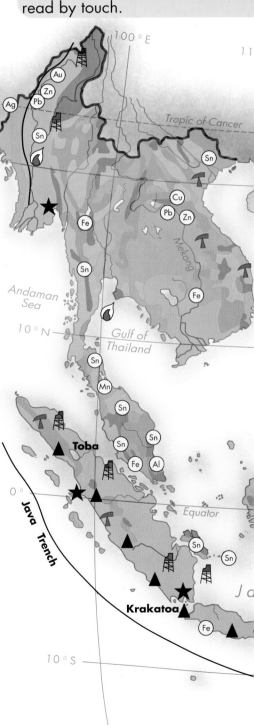

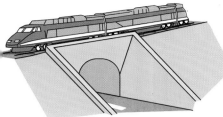

...ilway and embankment.

...he symbol showing railway
...d embankment on a map.

Line Symbols

These are used for roads, boundaries, rivers, and railroads. Often rivers are shown in blue and roads in black. Some line symbols represent things that exist on the ground, such as rivers, while others represent invisible lines such as boundaries. Line symbols may be continuous, interrupted, smooth, multiple, or irregular.

A river delta.

The delta of a river is shown on a map by using line symbols.

Area Symbols

Area symbols show such things as forests, deserts, crops, or grassland. They consist of patterns, symbols, color, or shading, used to indicate that a region has some common attribute. An area symbol is used uniformly over the area indicated.

Examples of forest shown using different techniques

Dot and line patterns	Symbols	Color

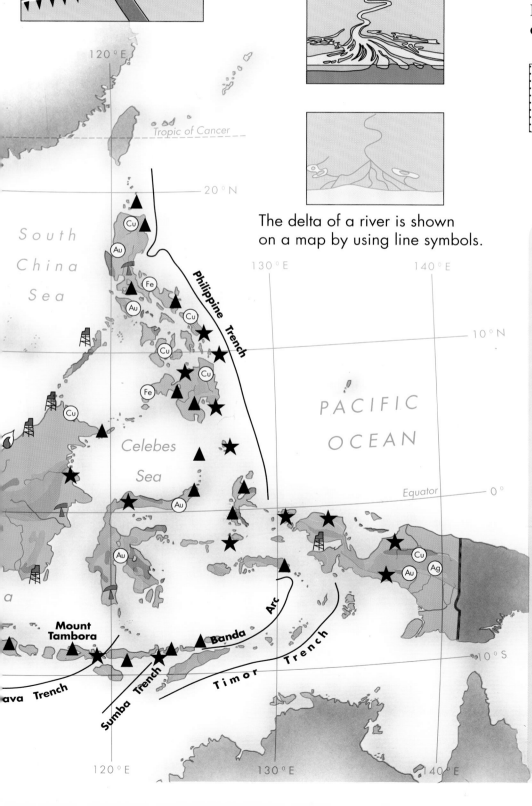

What the colors and symbols mean

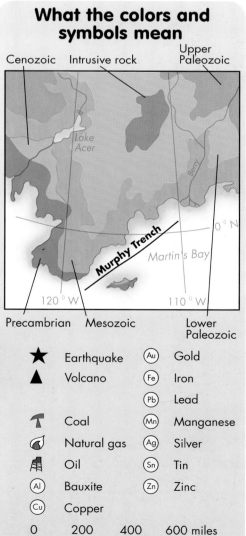

★	Earthquake	Au	Gold	
▲	Volcano	Fe	Iron	
		Pb	Lead	
⛏	Coal	Mn	Manganese	
◌	Natural gas	Ag	Silver	
⚒	Oil	Sn	Tin	
Al	Bauxite	Zn	Zinc	
Cu	Copper			

0   200   400   600 miles

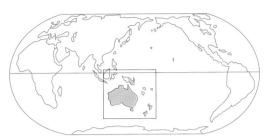

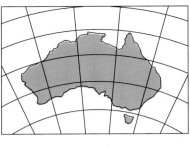

Azimuth

There is no perfect way of showing a round world on a flat piece of paper, and the problems are greater the bigger the area, such as Australia, being mapped. Most atlas map projections are compromises in some way.

Properties of Map Projections

The four main properties of map projections — area, shape, distance, and direction — are distorted in various ways and to different degrees by different projections.

Area

There are projections that enable the mapmaker to represent the areas of different regions in correct or constant proportion to what is actually on earth. Any square inch on the map represents an identical number of square miles anywhere else on the map. However, the shape of the area that is drawn is inevitably distorted. A square on earth may, for instance, become a rectangle on the map, but the rectangle has the correct area. These projections are known as equivalent or equal-area.

Shape

There is no projection that manages to provide correct shape for large areas, but some are able to portray the shapes of small areas by maintaining the correct angular relationships. Maps that have true shapes for small areas are called conformal. Parallels and meridians always intersect at right angles on these maps as they do on the globe. A map cannot be both conformal and equivalent at the same time.

Distance

Distance relationships are almost always subject to error on a map, but some projections do maintain true distances in one direction or along certain lines. Equidistant projections show true distances in all directions, but only from one or two central points. The planar equidistant projection is an example of this.

Direction

As for distances, directions on maps between all points cannot be shown without distortion. There are projections that allow the map user to measure correctly from one point to any other point.

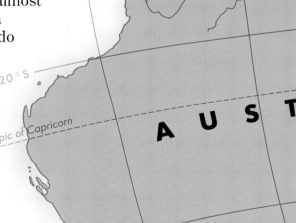

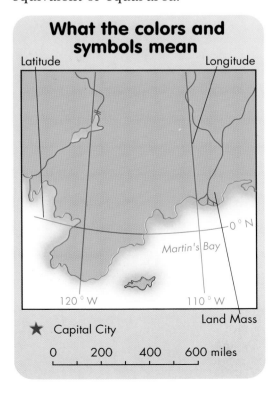

What the colors and symbols mean

Latitude Longitude

0° N

Martin's Bay

120° W   110° W

Land Mass

★ Capital City

0   200   400   600 miles

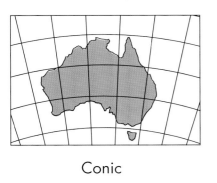

Conic

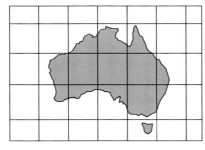

Mercator (Cylindrical)

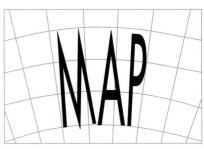

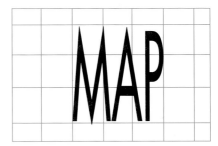

...ese different projections of ...ustralia above show just how ...fferent the maps can look. ...e first one is showing the ...me projection used for the map ... Australasia on these pages.

Using the grid of any projection, it is possible for you to experiment with how it can distort the shape of a face or letters, as shown in these examples.

Azimuthal projections distort the shape and the scale away from the focal point of the map.

Conic projections have a distortion of scale increasing with distance from the true latitude chosen when the map area is selected.

Mercator (Cylindrical) projections exaggerate areas as the distance from the equator increases. Notice that the poles can never be shown accurately because the meridians never meet.

PAPUA

NEW GUINEA

Gulf of
Papua

Solomon
Sea

Gulf of
...entaria

PACIFIC OCEAN

150° E

160° E

170° E

10° S

Coral Sea

L I A

20° S

Tropic of Capricorn

30° S

★ **Canberra**

T a s m a n   S e a

Bass Strait

180°

NEW

ZEALAND

40° S

140° E

150° E

160° E

170° E

180°

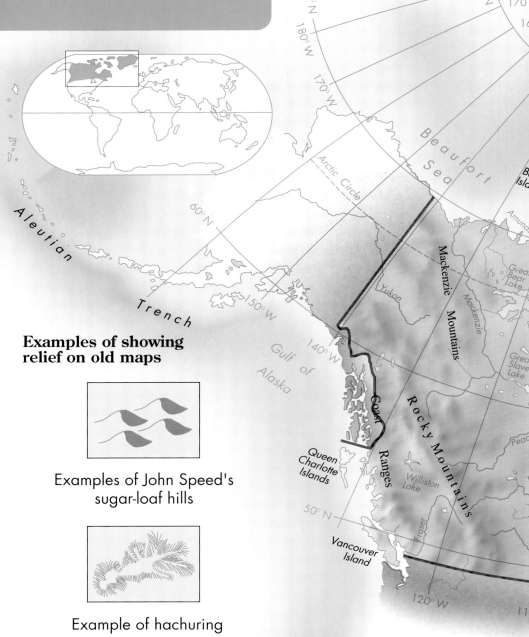

Physical maps, such as this one of Canada, show the terrain or the topography of a region. They can depict the surface features of a relatively small area, often with great accuracy. One of the main problems of drawing good physical maps is to represent the changes in height and depth that occur over the area in a clear and attractive way.

Relief

The difference in elevation between parts of the earth's surface is known as relief.

The elevation, or height, of any particular point can be measured and put on the map as a figure relating to a specific point. There is a limit to how many points and heights can be arranged on a map, and identifying the main mountains or hills may be all that is possible.

Landscape on Early Maps

Early maps, such as those of John Speed in the early 17th century, showed hilly land by drawing shapes like sugar loaves, shaded on one side. He made no attempt at vertical scale, but some effort was made to draw hills at relative heights. Later mapmakers used hill shading to show the shape and slope of the land. Lines were drawn down the sides of slopes. Steepness could be indicated by thickening the lines, but height was not easy to show. Ranges of hills sometimes looked rather like hairy caterpillars. The technique of hachuring, a more scientific form of hill shading, developed in the early 18th century, along with spot heights.

The contour method was first used by a Dutchman, N.S. Cruquius, to chart a riverbed in 1729. Contours were not used to show hills until well into the 19th century.

Examples of showing relief on old maps

Examples of John Speed's sugar-loaf hills

Example of hachuring

What the colors and symbols mean

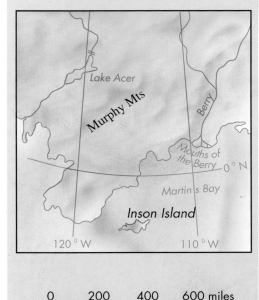

Shaded Relief

To increase the visual effect of a physical map, shaded relief is sometimes used. This gives the map an almost realistic three-dimensional surface. It can be explained by imagining a light source, usually in the northwest of the map, which illuminates a model of the whole area, creating the effect of sunlight and shadows. Parts that are shadowed are darkened on the map. This technique is particularly useful on topographic maps of small areas and is used on this map of Canada. Shaded relief makes these maps useful tools for people such as planners, developers, hikers, and casual users.

Map Labels

ARCTIC OCEAN

Greenland

Ellesmere Island

Queen Elizabeth Islands

Parry Islands

Devon I

Viscount Melville Sound

Lancaster Sound

Prince of Wales I

...ria Island

Somerset Island

Gulf of Boothia

Melville Peninsula

Baffin Island

Baffin Bay

Davis Strait

Denmark Strait

Arctic Circle

Cumberland Sound

Labrador Sea

Foxe Basin

Hudson Strait

Cape Chidley

Southampton Island

Ungava Peninsula

Ungava Bay

Labrador

Hudson Bay

Smallwood Reservoir

...basca

Reindeer Lake

Nelson

Severn

James Bay

Newfoundland

Gulf of Saint Lawrence

Saskatchewan

Lake Winnipeg

Lake Manitoba

St Lawrence

Ottawa

Lake Superior

Lake Michigan

Lake Ontario

Niagara Falls

Measuring the Surface of the Earth

People who measure the surface of the earth are called surveyors. The system they use to obtain their measurements is called triangulation.

Long ago, people discovered an important thing about triangles. If you know the length of one side and the size of two angles, you can work out the length of the other two sides.

A surveyor has to make just one accurate measurement of a straight line with a steel tape. This is often done along a road. The line is the first side of the triangle, called the base line. Next the surveyor locates a landmark — perhaps a tree. It is the tip of the triangle he now draws on his map. He measures the angles and figures out how long the other sides of the triangle are.

Then he locates a second landmark — perhaps a church spire. Using the same base line, he draws a second triangle with the spire at its top. Now just measuring the angles he can tell how far the tree is from the spire. From then on the surveyor locates new landmarks and draws new triangles. Triangle by triangle, surveyors have moved across continents, and their work is very accurate.

Aerial Photography

Mapping can be speeded up by taking photographs from planes with a special camera equipped with a stereoscopic device that can determine the exact slope and size of features such as mountains. Areas that are otherwise difficult to survey, such as deserts and mountains, can be mapped easily from the air.

...s the aircraft flies over the land, ...erial photographs are taken so ...at they overlap each other. ...irs of photographs are placed ...o a stereoscope, which enables ...e features on the photographs ...appear to stand out in three ...mensions.

Amazing – But True

★ Soon after the development of the camera, carrier pigeons wearing miniature cameras that took exposures automatically at set intervals were used to take aerial photographs of Paris.

Contours are the most accurate method of reproducing terrain, giving the map user information about the elevation of any place on the map and the size, shape, and slope of relief features.

Contours

The main way of showing elevation on physical maps is by using the contour line. This is a line that joins all points of equal elevation above a certain level, usually mean sea level. Contours are imaginary lines that can be thought of as the slices that would result if a series of progressively higher cuts were made through a vertical object. The diagram shows the relationship between the contour lines and the elevation of an island.

The contour interval is the spacing between contour lines. The map usually gives you the contour interval figure. In a relatively flat area the contour interval may be 5 feet. Intervals of 10 to 20 feet are often used.

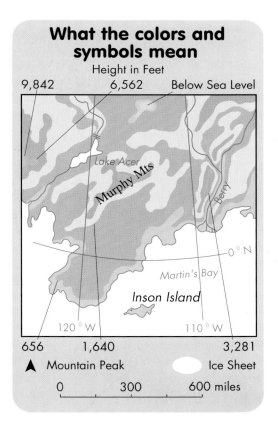

What the colors and symbols mean

Height in Feet

| 9,842 | 6,562 | Below Sea Level |

Lake Acer

Murphy Mts

Berry

0° N

Martin's Bay

Inson Island

120° W   110° W

| 656 | 1,640 | 3,281 |

▲ Mountain Peak   Ice Sheet

0   300   600 miles

In mountainous areas the contour interval is usually greater to help with the clarity of the map. Generally, the more irregular the surface, the more contour lines need to be drawn. The closer the contour lines are together, the steeper the slope.

Measuring the Height of Places Above Sea Level

Surveyors measure the heights of slopes, hills, and mountains. These measurements are taken with a kind of telescope and a stick marked with red and white bands.

How to Draw a Cross Section

Draw a cross section using the contour map of the Commonwealth of Independent States. An example has been drawn showing the cross section between the points A and on this map. Choose another two points on this map and draw your own cross section.

60° N   70° N

Norwegian Sea

50° N

Svalbard

Bear Island

Arctic Circle

Baltic Sea

Gulf of Finland

Kola Peninsula

Kolguyev I.

White Sea

20° E

Lake Ladoga

Lake Onega

Northern Dvina

Pechora

Volga

Rybinsk Res.

Kuybyshev Res.

Kama

Ural Mountains

Sea of Azov

Black Sea

Volga

Ural

Mt Elbrus
18,510ft

Caspian Sea

Kirgiz Steppe

Ust - Urt Plateau

Aral Sea

40° N

40° E

Kara Kum

60° E

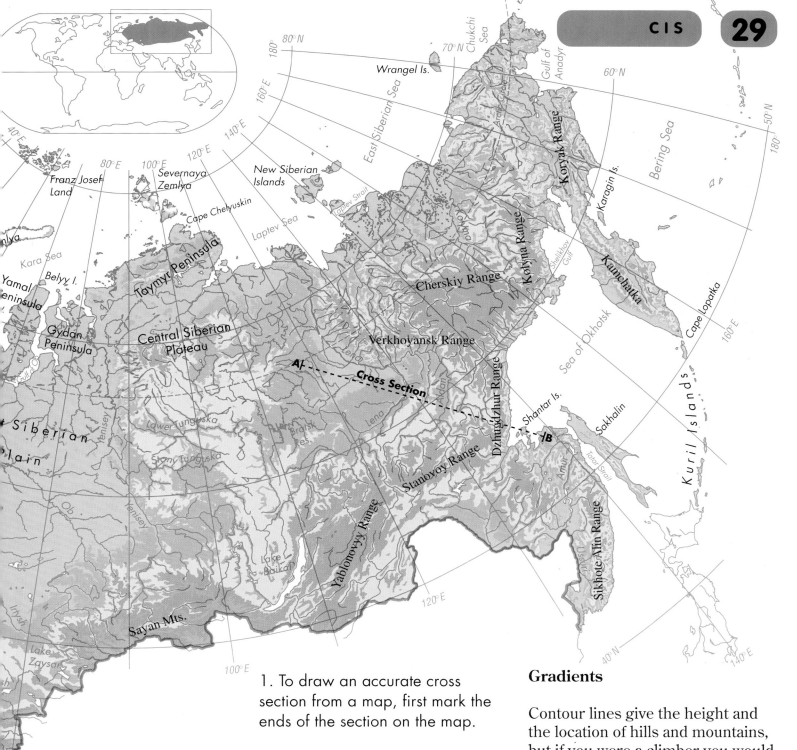

Gradients

Contour lines give the height and the location of hills and mountains, but if you were a climber you would want to know if the slope was steep or gentle. This is known as the gradient. The gradient of a slope between two points is obtained by dividing the rise between the two points by the horizontal distance between them. If the rise is 50 feet and the distance is 500 feet, that is 50 divided by 500, which is 1/10 or 1 in 10. Some gradients of interest:
1 in 15 — too steep for most cyclists.
1 in 5 — very steep: cars need a low gear.
1 in 3 — too steep for ordinary vehicles: a steep climb for walkers.
1 in 1 — appears vertical.

1. To draw an accurate cross section from a map, first mark the ends of the section on the map.

2. Take a piece of paper and lay it along the line joining the two points. Mark each contour that crosses the paper. Number the contours according to their height as you work along the line.

3. Lay your paper along a line drawn on another piece of paper and transfer your points to the correct height on the framework. Join the points together.

4. It helps to mark any key points such as mountains or rivers.

Cross Section

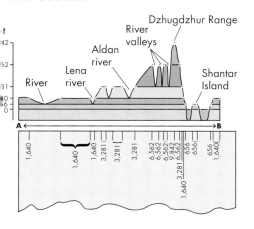

In order to draw a map of any area it is necessary to reduce or scale it down so that it can be represented on a sheet of paper or an atlas page. The scale of a map is the ratio of the measurement of something on a map and the corresponding measurement on earth.

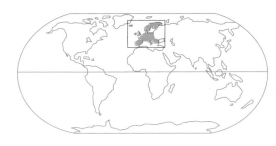

Scale

Scale is usually expressed in one of three ways:

1. As a representative fraction (RF), which can be expressed as a fraction or a ratio. The first number represents the map distance, the second the actual distance. Any unit can be used as long as the same unit is used for both figures. So if the scale was 1/50,000, it could also be given as 1:50,000 — one unit on the map is equal to 50,000 on the ground. Numerical scales are the most accurate of scale measurements and can be understood in any language.

RF 1:24,000

RF 1:2,000,000

RF 1:25,000,000

2. By verbal statement, such as 1 inch to 1 mile. This means that one inch on the map is equal to one mile on the ground.

One inch represents 2,000 feet

One inch represents approximately 32 miles

One inch represents approximately 400 miles

3. By linear scale, which is a horizontal line divided into sections, each of which represents a unit of measurement on the ground.

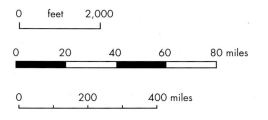

The Map Index

The map index helps to locate places on a map. It lists the features shown on a map in alphabetical order, giving a grid reference.

Using grid line numbers, a location can be given for any place on a map. The way this is done is to quote the number of the line to the west of the point and then the number of the line to the south. You can do this even more accurately if you imagine each square is divided into tenths.

The first set of figures are called the eastings and the second set the northings.

Physical/Political Map

The map of Europe on this page is a standard physical map with political information laid over the top of the physical detail. You can see which cities and towns are located in areas of high relief.

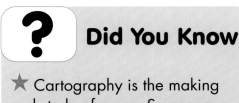

? **Did You Know**

★ Cartography is the making and study of maps. Someone who draws maps is a cartographer.

What the colors and symbols mean

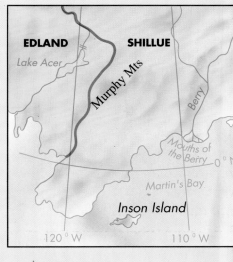

★ Capital City

| 0 | 200 | 400 | 600 miles |

How to Draw a Map or Plan

If you look down from above on an everyday object such as a table, you can draw the object from above. The same is true if you look down on an area such as your backyard from an upstairs window. You can draw a plan or outline of the yard.

To help you be more exact, draw squares on the map and make a grid. Write letters along the bottom of the grid and numbers along the side. The letters and numbers can be used to name each square on the grid. The grid squares can help you locate exactly where every feature of your backyard is positioned.

But how far is it from one end of the yard to the other? In order for your map or plan to give accurate information, it must be correct to start with. This means that each distance and object will have to be carefully measured and sized before it is placed on the plan.

Draw a scale bar along the base of your plan, and use it to draw your sizes correctly.

2. Looking directly down at the desk, it is now possible to see all the objects. As it shows only the outlines of the objects seen on the desk, this drawing is called a plan. Can you accurately describe the position of the ruler?.

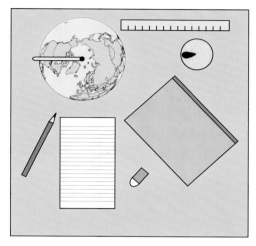

3. By drawing straight lines over the plan it is divided into squares and makes a grid. If letters are added along the top and numbers down the side of the plan, each square can be named by a number and a letter. Now it is possible to accurately describe the position of the ruler as starting in 1C and ending in 1F.

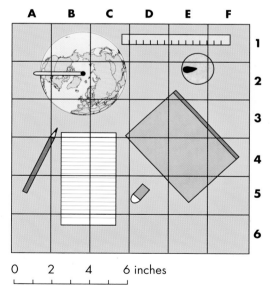

1. Look at this picture of a desk with a selection of objects. You can see most of the objects, but one is partially hidden.

Name the grid square in which the eraser can be found.

It is important to remember that a map is really a plan of an area of land. The map grid is made up by the lines of latitude and longitude.

e Grid System

ou look for a place on a globe or orld map you use lines of gitude and latitude for reference, t it is not possible to use these on ps drawn to a large scale. Grid es are used instead, a system of tical and horizontal lines that ide the map into squares.

Distances on maps can be worked out by using the scale line. If you put a strip of paper next to the scale line on the map and mark off the miles shown, you can make your own scale ruler with which to move over the map and measure distances.

Use of Different Scales for Different Needs

Maps are drawn at many different scales. A large-scale map would be for a small area where considerable detail was required, such as a town plan or a small country area. For example, a 1:600 (1 inch to 600 inches or 50 feet) would be able to feature buildings and roads drawn to scale. Small-scale maps, such as those drawn for countries or continents, would have a far smaller ratio, such as one inch to 100 or even 1,000 miles (1:6,336,000 or 1:63,360,000).

Illustrated here are three samples of maps. In each one the same city, Copenhagen, is shown, but as we go down the page the scale becomes smaller as the area represented becomes bigger. The first map is the smallest scale and the third is the largest.

Map 1. Scale of map is 1:15,000,000 --- one inch represents 237 miles. Denmark, the country that Copenhagen is the capital of, is shown relative to other countries in northern Europe.
Map 2. Scale of map is 1:5,000,000 — one inch represents 79 miles. Copenhagen is shown by a spot, and the position of Copenhagen within Denmark can be seen.
Map 3. Scale of the map is 1:1,500,000 —one inch represents 24 miles. The roads in Copenhagen can be seen at this scale, and distance can be measured using the scale bar.

Map 1

0   200   400 miles

inches
millimetres
30 29 28 27 26

Map 2

0 20 40 60 80 100 miles

inches
millimetres
30 29 28 27 26

Map 3

0   10   20   30   40 miles

inches
millimetres
30 29 28 27 26

? Did You Know

★ On a globe, distances, area, and direction can be observed without the distortion caused by projections used for flat maps.

What the colors and symbols mean

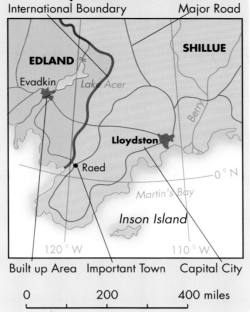

International Boundary — Major Road

EDLAND
Evadkin
Lake Acer
SHILLUE
Berry
Lloydston
Raed
0° N
Martin's Bay
Inson Island
120° W 110° W

Built up Area — Important Town — Capital City

0   200   400 miles

! Amazing – But True

★ The Langlois globe, produced in France in 1824, is thought to be the largest globe in the world, as it measures 128 feet in diameter. Most globes measure 22 inches in diameter.

Measuring Distances on Maps or Plans

You can use a scale ruler, a piece of paper, or a piece of string to measure distance. In this instance a piece of string has been used. This can help you to use the scale bar to convert the measurements along a winding road on maps into the actual distance they are on the ground.

1. Choose the places on the map you want to find the distances between. In this example the distance between Paris and Toulouse by road was chosen.

2. Place a piece of string on the map and use it to follow the roads between Paris and Toulouse. With a felt-tipped pen mark on the string the two towns you want to find the distance between.

3. Then place the string next to the scale bar, taking care to make sure the first mark is lined up with 0 on the scale bar. See how far the distance between the two marks is in miles.

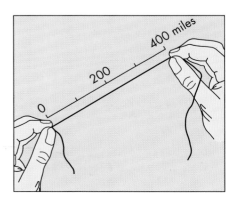

Graphs and diagrams serve a very useful purpose in cartography because they can provide information in a visual form and make it seem a lot more interesting or a lot less complicated. Look at diagrams closely, and notice whether quantities are shown in number or percentage terms. Scale is important in graphs and diagrams, and they should be precise so that exact information can be read from them. Identify relationships expressed between the elements, and observe the processes they describe.

Proportional Circles or Other Symbols

Comparing the amounts or quantities in different places or at different times can be well illustrated by drawing proportional areas.

Top producers of cotton in bales

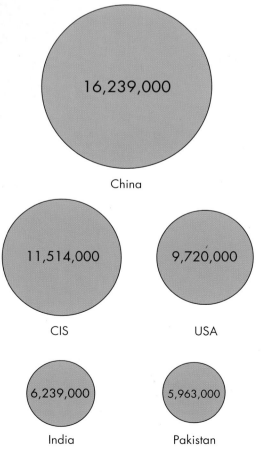

16,239,000
China

11,514,000
CIS

9,720,000
USA

6,239,000
India

5,963,000
Pakistan

Line graphs

A line graph is a diagram using two axes at right angles to each other. These graphs are very good for expressing the relationship between time and the change in some variable. A line graph would show clearly, for example, the growth in world population.

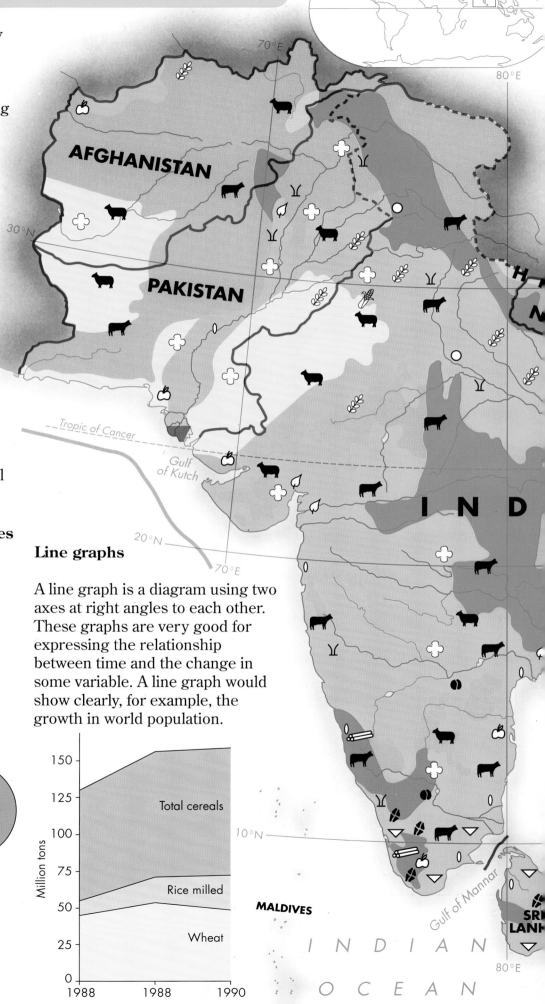

Million tons

150
125
100
75
50
25
0

Total cereals

Rice milled

Wheat

1988   1988   1990

AFGHANISTAN

PAKISTAN

Tropic of Cancer

Gulf
of Kutch

30°N

20°N

70°E

70°E

80°E

10°N

80°E

I N D

MALDIVES

Gulf of Mannar

SRI
LANK

I N D I A N

O C E A N

Bar Graphs

These very simple diagrams consist of a number of rectangular boxes, each a length proportional to the statistics represented. It is also possible to show statistics as a compound bar graph where one bar is split up into different proportions to illustrate the statistical breakdown. These diagrams can be used to show any number of things, such as main producers of a grain.

Top rice producers in tons

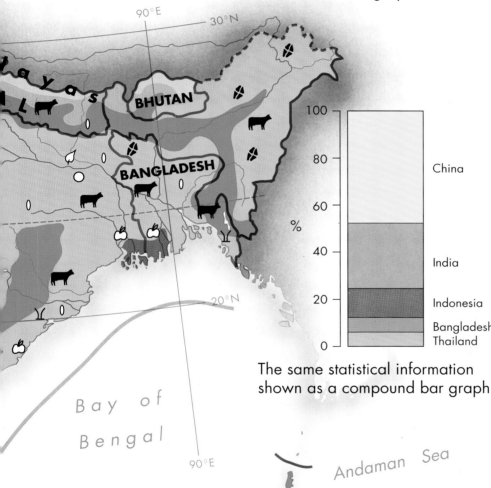

Shown as a bar graph

The same statistical information shown as a compound bar graph

Pie Charts

These are circles divided into sectors, and the circle represents the total value. Each sector is a proportion within the total circle. These are very good at showing the relative importance of different elements of a whole.

Top producers of potatoes

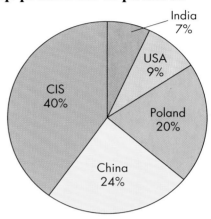

India 7%
USA 9%
Poland 20%
China 24%
CIS 40%

What the colors and symbols mean

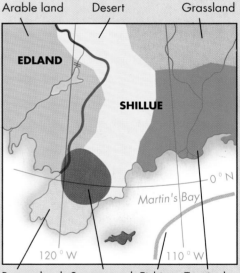

Arable land   Desert   Grassland

EDLAND

SHILLUE

Barren land   Swamp and   Fishing   Tropical
              Marshland   limit   rain forest

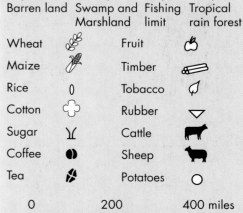

Wheat		Fruit	
Maize		Timber	
Rice		Tobacco	
Cotton		Rubber	
Sugar		Cattle	
Coffee		Sheep	
Tea		Potatoes	

0   200   400 miles

Amazing – But True

⭐ Pakistan was created from the northwestern and northeastern parts of India on August 14, 1947. Disputes over the boundary resulted in much fighting. The current boundary follows the Simla Agreement of 1972, although Kashmir still remains a disputed territory.

Maps that emphasize the boundaries of counties, states, countries, or continents are called political maps. They usually include the capital cities of each country. Political maps need to be colored carefully so that the shape of each individual country stands out.

Boundaries

Boundaries are the borders or limits of an area. Sometimes two countries get together and decide on their dividing line quite amicably. The line might be the top of a mountain ridge or a river. Surveyors may be employed to mark out a straight line.

Even when the sea marks the edge of a country, officials may have different interpretations of where the boundary lies. Some claim that the boundary extends 3 miles out into the water, others claim 12 miles.

War has decided many boundaries over the years. Conquerors have moved boundaries to suit themselves. The African countries in particular have many strange shapes. Most of these were carved out by European rulers, rather than decided by the Africans who lived in the countries. The discrepancy between tribal boundaries and national boundaries in Africa has led to a great deal of ethnic diversity in all countries.

Geometric Boundaries

Artificial boundaries are often sections of parallels of latitude or meridians of longitude. The western portion of the United States–Canada border that follows the 49th parallel is an example of one of these.

Natural Boundaries

Natural boundaries are based on physical features such as mountains, rivers, and lakes. Although they seem to be obvious boundaries, they often prove to be unsatisfactory. International boundaries along mountain ranges are not uncommon. The Alps, the Andes, and the Himalayas have mountain boundaries, and they have not always proved to be stable. Although the height of the mountains seems a barrier, tunnels, passes, and roads generally cross them. High pastures may be used for grazing and the source of water for hydroelectric power. Nor is it easy to define the boundary. Do you follow the crests or the water divide? Border disputes between China and India have partly been the result of these two features failing to coincide.

Rivers can be even more difficult as boundaries. The River Rhine is a boundary but also a traffic route. It is lined with factories and power stations and dotted with historic buildings. It is really more of a resource than a boundary. Where does the boundary lie? On the left or right bank, or down the center? Suppose a river changes course? The Mississippi River has often changed its route. The rule that is generally applied is that if the river changes its course quickly the old boundaries remain.

Over the last hundred years the Rio Grande has cut a new channel; each time a few acres of Mexican land have ended up on the United States side of the river, and the United States has claimed it. Mexico has not been happy about this and insisted that a rule about quickly changing rivers be applied. This was agreed upon in 1963, and now a small part of Mexico is situated north of the Rio Grande.

Disputed Boundaries

Disputed boundaries are still one of the most common sources of international conflict. Since World War II almost half of the world's sovereign states have been engaged in border disputes with neighboring countries. These may be positional disputes over the interpretation of the documents that define a boundary, or territorial disputes over the ownership of the region as a whole.

When a boundary has been superimposed on a country, dividing ethnically similar populations, disputes may arise. The Balkans are a good example of such a dispute.

In recent years in the Middle East, bitter wars have been fought about Israel's borders. Saudi Arabia has had border disputes with Yemen, and Iran and Iraq have fought a lengthy war over their boundaries.

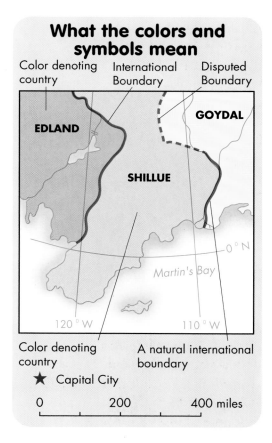

What the colors and symbols mean

Color denoting country — International Boundary — Disputed Boundary

EDLAND

GOYDAL

SHILLUE

Martin's Bay

Color denoting country — A natural international boundary

★ Capital City

0   200   400 miles

Practically anything can be used to make an effective map, and in Oceania the most abundant materials at hand are shells and sticks. In the past these have been arranged to create a map of the area by using the shells to represent the islands and the sticks to give the distance between each island.

Maps range in size from tiny portrayals that appear on postage stamps to the enormous logistical war maps used by the military to keep track of events during a war.

20°N

Northern Mariana Is.
(USA)

Guam
(USA)

10°N

Caroline Islands

Pacific Islands,
Trust Territory
(USA)

Wake Island
(USA)

Marshall
Islands

Marshall Is.
(USA)

PACIFIC

OCEAN

Micronesia

Melanesia

Federated States
of Micronesia
(USA)

Gilbert
Islands

NAURU

Equator

0°

Arafura Sea

Solomon Sea

SOLOMON ISLANDS

TUVALU

Gulf of
Papua

10°S

Coral
Sea

VANUATU

FIJI

20°S

New Caledonia
(Fr.)

Tropic of Capricorn

140°E

150°E

160°E

170°E

30°S

? **Did You Know**

★ The Southern Hemisphere has more water than the Northern Hemisphere.

150°E

160°E

170°E

What the colors and symbols mean

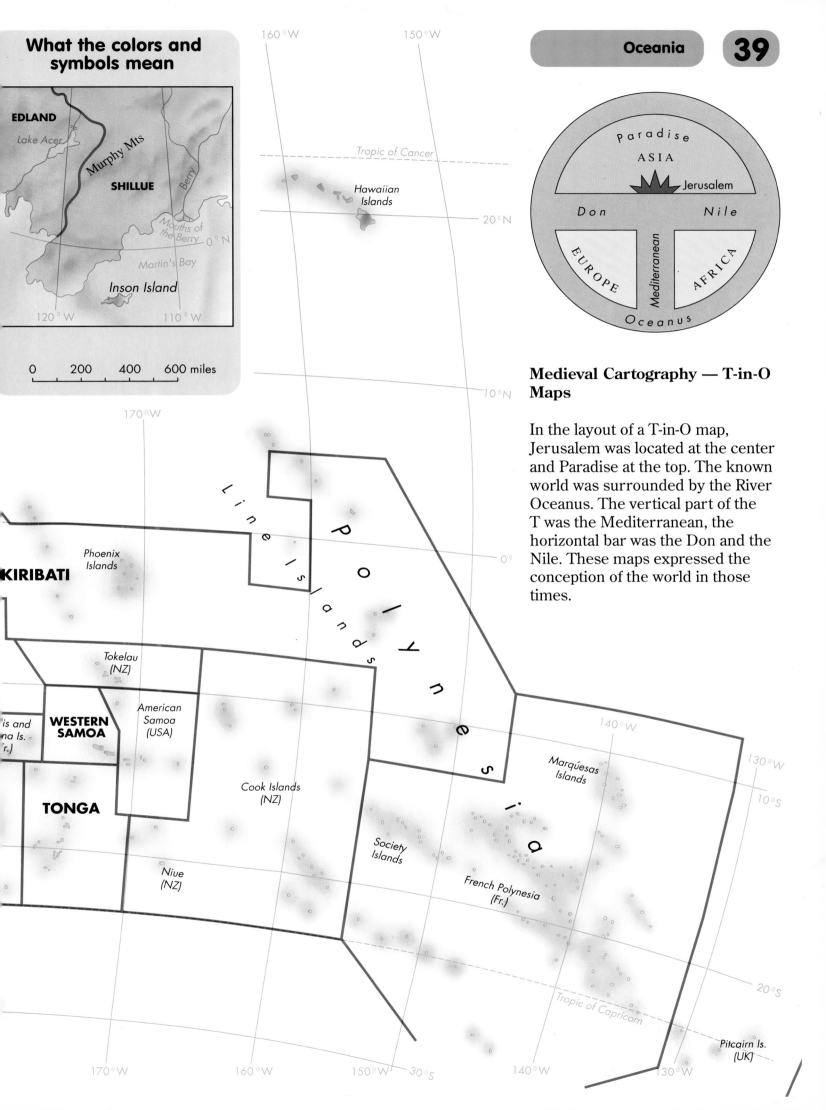

EDLAND

Lake Acer

Murphy Mts

SHILLUE

Berry

Mouths of the Berry

Martin's Bay

0° N

Inson Island

120° W   110° W

0   200   400   600 miles

Tropic of Cancer

160° W   150° W   20° N   10° N   0°

Hawaiian Islands

170° W

Line Islands

Phoenix Islands

KIRIBATI

P o l y n e s i a

Tokelau (NZ)

140° W   130° W   10° S

WESTERN SAMOA

American Samoa (USA)

is and na Is. (Fr.)

Cook Islands (NZ)

Marquesas Islands

TONGA

Niue (NZ)

Society Islands

French Polynesia (Fr.)

20° S

Tropic of Capricorn

170° W   160° W   150° W   30° S   140° W   130° W

Pitcairn Is. (UK)

Medieval Cartography — T-in-O Maps

In the layout of a T-in-O map, Jerusalem was located at the center and Paradise at the top. The known world was surrounded by the River Oceanus. The vertical part of the T was the Mediterranean, the horizontal bar was the Don and the Nile. These maps expressed the conception of the world in those times.

Paradise

ASIA

Jerusalem

Don   Nile

EUROPE   Mediterranean   AFRICA

Oceanus

Many nations have come to assume their present shape as a result of growth over centuries of time. They grew outward from a central region into surrounding territory. The original core area often contains the largest cities and densest population.This is true of London, the Paris basin, and the northeastern United States.

Capital City

The capital city of a country is usually situated within its core region and is often the focus of it. It is dominant because it is the seat of central authority and government, but is often the center of economic functions as well. Paris in France, London in the United Kingdom, and Mexico City are all examples of political, economic, and cultural centers.

Such capitals are common in countries with highly centralized governments, few internal cultural contrasts, a strong sense of national identity, and well-defined borders. Most European capitals are of this type. Newly independent countries whose former colonial occupiers established a main center of administration also have a core capital city.

In federal states, which are associations of more or less equal states or provinces with strong regional government, the capital city may have been created to serve as an administrative center. Ottawa in Canada and Canberra in Australia are examples. A capital city located in the center of the country enables a government to assert its authority more easily. Many capital cities, such as Washington, D.C., were centrally located when they were designated the capital but lost their central position as the nation expanded.

!

Amazing – But True

★ In the Christian Science building in Boston, it is possible to stand inside a globe and see the outlines of the earth's surface.

Relocated Capitals

A special type of relocated capital is called a forward-thrust capital city. These are relocated specifically to signal a government's awareness of regions away from its core.

Brazil moved its capital from Rio de Janeiro to the new city of Brasilia in the 1950s to show its intent to develop the interior of the country.

Divided Capitals

In some countries, two cities share government functions. Divided capitals are found in South Africa, the Netherlands, and Bolivia.

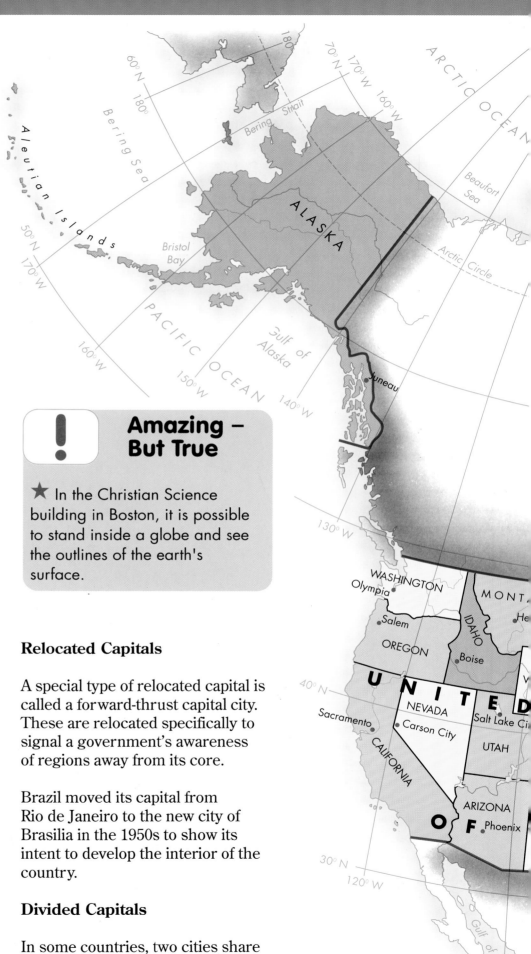

[C]olor on Maps

[C]olor allows much greater detail to [be] shown on maps. It adds visual [in]terest and increases the ability to [sh]ow a hierarchy or structure [be]cause color may be used to code [th]ings that are similar or dissimilar.

[H]ow many colors do you need [on] a map?

[Su]rprising as it may seem, no map [i]s ever needed more than four [co]lors. Suppose you want to draw a [m]ap where no two states bordering [ea]ch other have the same color. [M]athematicians do not know why, [bu]t the solution can be achieved [wi]th just four colors.

? Did You Know

★ Wildly conflicting physical maps did not help either side in the American Civil War. In 1862 the Union army planned to capture the Confederates' capital swiftly, but unexpected obstacles slowed their advance. The Confederates would have been able to overwhelm the Union troops if they had had an accurate map.

★ Nazi cartographers tried to persuade the United States to remain neutral by drawing spheres of influence on a map. They meant to influence the Americans to stay in their sphere and not to interfere with events in Europe.

The Main Skills of Map Reading

 1. Locating places using latitude and longitude or grid references

 2. Working out direction using the points of a compass

 3. Calculating distances by using the map scale

 4. Recognizing map symbols — i.e. naming a feature shown by the symbol

 5. Working out gradient or slope

 6. Identifying areas of different height

 7. Recognizing physical and human map features

 8. Drawing a cross section

 Clues are given in Legends, Indexes, Geographic Grids, and Scales

What the colors and symbols mean

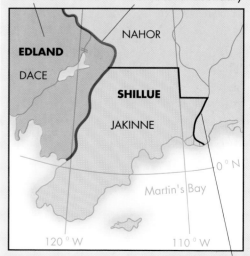

Color denotes state   International Boundary

EDLAND
DACE
NAHOR
SHILLUE
JAKINNE
Martin's Bay

State Boundary

★ Capital City   • State Capital

0   200   400   600 miles

NORTH DAKOTA
• Bismarck
MINNESOTA
SOUTH DAKOTA
• Pierre
St. Paul
WISCONSIN
• Madison
MICHIGAN
Lansing
MAINE
• Augusta
VERMONT
Montpelier
NEW HAMPSHIRE
Concord
Boston
MASSACHUSETTS
RHODE ISLAND
Providence
Hartford
CONNECTICUT
NEBRASKA
IOWA
• Des Moines
ILLINOIS
Springfield
Indianapolis
OHIO
Columbus
PENNSYLVANIA
Harrisburg
NEW YORK
Albany
NEW JERSEY
Trenton
Dover
DELAWARE
Washington D.C.
MARYLAND
Cheyenne
Lincoln
Topeka
KANSAS
Jefferson City
INDIANA
Frankfort
MISSOURI
KENTUCKY
Nashville
WEST VIRGINIA
Charleston
Richmond
VIRGINIA
Raleigh
NORTH CAROLINA
Denver
STATES
Santa Fe
OKLAHOMA
Oklahoma City
ARKANSAS
Little Rock
TENNESSEE
Columbia
SOUTH CAROLINA
ATLANTIC OCEAN
AMERICA
MISSISSIPPI
Jackson
ALABAMA
Montgomery
GEORGIA
Atlanta
Tallahassee
FLORIDA
TEXAS
• Austin
Baton Rouge
LOUISIANA
Gulf of Mexico
Straits of Florida
Tropic of Cancer
100   90   80   50° N   70° W   40° N   30°   90° W   80° W

Astronomer
A person who studies the science of celestial bodies — the sun, the moon, the planets, the stars and the galaxies, and all other objects in the universe.

Cartographers
People who practice the art and technique of compiling and drawing maps and charts.

Chronometer
A timepiece designed to tell the time accurately in all conditions of pressure and temperature — especially at sea.

Concentric Circles
Circles of different sizes that all have the same center.

Conformal Map Projections
Those in which the shape of small areas are accurately portrayed.

Contours
Lines drawn on maps along which all points are of equal height above or below sea level.

Distortion
A change in the representation or shape of something so that it is not accurately portrayed.

Elevation
The height of something above a given place, usually sea level.

Equidistant Map Projections
Those on which the true distances in all directions can be measured from one or two central points.

Equivalent Map Projections
Those on which all areas of regions are represented in correct proportion. Also called Equal-Area Projections.

Gradient
The slope or inclination of a road, railway, or path. The ratio between the vertical distance between two points and the horizontal distance between them is a measure of gradient. Also called grade.

Graticule
The intersecting lines of latitude and longitude on which a map is drawn.

Gyrocompass
A nonmagnetic compass that uses a motor-driven gyroscope to indicate true north.

Hachuring
Shading on a relief map consisting of short lines that indicate gradient.

Latitude
A measure of the distance north or south of the equator, given in degrees.

Longitude
A measure of the distance east or west of the prime meridian, given in degrees.

Meridians
The north-south lines of longitude on the globe. Meridians are all of equal length and meet at the poles.

Orientation
The adjustment or alignment of a map in relation to a compass or other directions.

Parallels
The east-west lines of latitude that indicate distance north or south of the equator.

Rhumb Line
A line of constant compass bearing; it cuts all meridians at the same angle.

Scale
In mapping, scale is the ratio between the length or size of an area on a map and the actual length or size of the same area on the earth's surface.

Solstice
Either the shortest day of the year (winter solstice) or the longest day of the year (summer solstice).

Stereoscopic Camera
One used for creating two-dimensional pictures, giving a representation of depth and relief.

Triangulation
The method of surveying an area by dividing it up into triangles. One side, the base line, and all angles are measured, and the lengths of the other lines are then calculated.

Arnold, Caroline. *Maps and Globes.*
New York: Watts, 1984.

Baynes, John. *How Maps Are Made.*
New York: Facts on File, 1987.

Blandford, Percy W. *Maps and Compasses.*
2nd ed. Blue Ridge Summit, PA: Tab Books, 1992.

Campbell, John. *Introductory Cartography.*
Englewood Cliffs, NJ: Prentice Hall, 1984.

Carey, Helen H. *How To Use Maps and Globes.*
New York: Watts, 1983.

Keates, J. S. *Understanding Maps.*
New York: Wiley, 1982.

Lambert, David. *Maps and Globes.*
New York: Bookwright Press, 1987.

Kjellstrom, Bjorn. *Be Expert with Map and Compass.*
New York: Scribner's, 1976.

Lye, Keith. *Measuring and Maps.*
New York: Gloucester Press, 1991.

Mango, Karin. *Map-Making.*
New York: Julian Messner, 1984.

Monmonier, Mark. *How To Lie with Maps.*
Chicago: University of Chicago Press, 1991.

Weiss, Harvey. *Maps.*
Boston: Houghton Mifflin, 1991.

Westfall, Claude Z. *Basic Graphics and Cartography.*
Orono: University of Maine at Orono Press, 1984.

This index is designed to help you to find places shown on the maps. The index is in alphabetical order and lists all towns, countries, and physical features. After each entry extra information is given to describe the entry and to tell you which country or continent it is in.

The next column contains the latitude and longitude figures. These are used to help locate places on maps. They are measured in degrees. The blue lines drawn across the map are lines of latitude. The equator is at latitude 0°. All lines above the equator are referred to as °N (north of the equator). All lines below the equator are referred to as °S (south of the equator).

The blue lines drawn from the top to the bottom of the map are lines of longitude. The 0° line passes through Greenwich, London, and is known as the Greenwich Meridian. All lines of longitude join the North Pole to the South Pole. All lines to the right of the Greenwich Meridian are referred to as °E (east of Greenwich), and all lines to the left of the Greenwich Meridian are referred to as °W (west of Greenwich).

The final column indicates the number of the page where you will find the place for which you are searching.

If you want to find out where the Gulf of Thailand is, look it up in the alphabetical index. The entry will read:

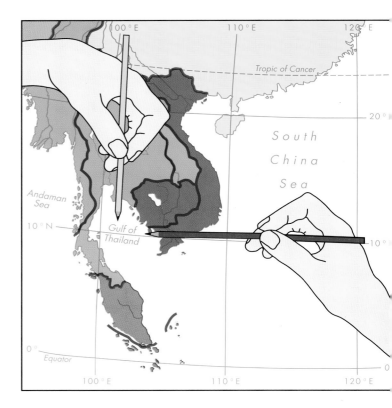

Name, Description	Location		Page
	Lat.	Long.	
Thailand, Gulf of, Asia	11°N	101°E	22

Turn to page 22 in your atlas. The Gulf of Thailand is located where latitude 11°N meets longitude 101°E. Place a pencil along latitude 11°N. Now take another pencil and place it along 101°E. Where the two pencils meet is the location of the Gulf of Thailand. Practice finding places in the index and on the maps.

Name, Description	Location		Page
	Lat.	Long.	
A			
Abu Dhabi, capital of United Arab Emirates	24°N	54°E	37
Afghanistan, country in Asia	33°N	65°E	34
Alabama, state in United States	33°N	87°W	41
Alaska, Gulf of, North America	59°N	145°W	40
Alaska, state in United States	65°N	150°W	40
Albania, country in Europe	41°N	20°E	31
Albany, state capital of New York	43°N	74°W	41
Aldan, river in Asia	60°N	133°E	29
Aleutian Islands, Pacific Ocean	52°N	175°W	40
Alps, mountain range in Europe	46°N	10°E	30
American Samoa, island group in Pacific Ocean	14°S	170°W	39
Amman, capital of Jordan	32°N	36°E	36
Amsterdam, capital of Netherlands	52°N	5°E	33
Amundsen Sea, Antarctica	75°S	110°W	18
Amur, river in Asia	52°N	130°E	29
Anadyr, Gulf of, Asia	65°N	181°W	29
Andaman Sea, Indian Ocean	11°N	96°E	35
Andes, mountain range in South America	20°S	70°W	16
Andorra, country in Europe	43°N	2°E	32
Ankara, capital of Turkey	40°N	32°E	36
Antwerp, city in Belgium	51°N	4°E	33
Arabian Sea, Indian Ocean	18°N	60°E	37
Arafura Sea, Southeast Asia	9°S	135°E	24
Aral Sea, Asia	45°N	60°E	28
Århus, city in Denmark	56°N	10°E	33
Arizona, state in United States	35°N	112°W	40
Arkansas, state in United States	35°N	92°W	41
Athabasca, Lake, North America	59°N	109°W	27
Athabasca, river in North America	58°N	113°W	26
Athens, capital of Greece	38°N	24°E	31
Atlanta, state capital of Georgia	34°N	84°W	41
Augusta, state capital of Maine	44°N	69°W	41
Austin, state capital of Texas	30°N	98°W	41
Australia, continent and country	23°S	135°E	24
Austria, country in Europe	48°N	15°E	33
Azov, Sea of, Asia	46°N	36°E	28
B			
Baffin Bay, North America	72°N	65°W	27
Baffin Island, North America	66°N	70°W	27
Baghdad, capital of Iraq	33°N	45°E	36
Bahamas, island country in Atlantic Ocean	25°N	78°W	15
Bahrain, country in Middle East	26°N	51°E	37
Baikal, Lake, Asia	54°N	108°E	29
Balearic Islands, Mediterranean Sea	40°N	3°W	32
Balkhash, Lake, Asia	46°N	74°E	28
Baltic Sea, Europe	56°N	20°E	31

74393   72U8G

T

Tagus, river in Europe	39°N	8°W	30
Taiwan, island country in Asia	23°N	121°E	21
Tallahassee, state capital of Florida	31°N	84°W	41
Tambora, Mount, a volcano in Southeast Asia	9°S	118°E	23
Tanganyika, Lake, southeast Africa	7°S	30°E	13
Tasman Sea, Pacific Ocean	35°S	160°E	25
Taymyr Lake, Asia	74°N	102°E	29
Teheran, capital of Iran	36°N	51°E	37
Tennessee, state in United States	36°N	87°W	41
Texas, state in United States	32°N	100°W	41
Thailand, Gulf of, Southeast Asia	11°N	101°E	22
Timor Sea, southeast Asia	10°S	128°E	25
Tiranë, capital of Albania	41°N	20°E	31
Toba, a volcano in Southeast Asia	3°S	103°E	22
Tokelau Islands, island group in Pacific Ocean	8°S	172°W	39
Topeka, state capital of Kansas	39°N	96°W	41
Trenton, state capital of New Jersey	40°N	75°W	41
Turkey, country in Europe and Asia	39°N	35°E	36
Tuvalu, island country in Pacific Ocean	8°S	178°W	38

U

Ungava Bay, North America	59°N	69°W	27
Ungava Peninsula, North America	60°N	75°W	27
United Arab Emirates, country in Middle East	23°N	54°E	37
United Kingdom, country in Europe	53°N	2°W	32
United States of America, country in North America	40°N	100°W	41
Ural, river in Europe and Asia	49°N	52°E	28
Ural Mountains, Europe and Asia	60°N	59°E	28
Ussuri, river in Asia	46°N	135°E	29
Ust-Urt Plateau, Asia	44°N	55°E	28
Utah, state in United States	40°N	111°W	40

V

Valletta, capital of Malta	36°N	14°E	33
Vancouver Island, North America	50°N	126°W	26
Vanuatu, island country in Pacific Ocean	16°S	168°W	38
Vatican City, independent state in Italy	42°N	12°E	33
Vaygach Island, Kara Sea	70°N	60°E	28
Venice, city in Italy	45°N	12°E	33
Verkhoyansk Range, Asia	66°N	128°E	29
Vermont, state in United States	44°N	73°W	41
Victoria, Lake, east central Africa	1°S	33°E	13
Victoria Island, North America	71°N	110°W	27
Vienna, capital of Austria	48°N	16°E	33
Virginia, state in United States	38°N	79°W	41
Vistula, river in Europe	57°N	20°E	31
Volga, river in Europe	48°N	47°E	28

W

Wake Island, Pacific Ocean	19°N	167°E	38
Wallis and Futuna, island group in Pacific Ocean	13°S	177°W	38
Warsaw, capital of Poland	52°N	21°E	31
Washington, DC, capital of United States of America	39°N	77°W	41
Washington, state in United States	48°N	120°W	41
Weddell Sea, Antarctica	67°S	45°W	18
West Indies, island group in Caribbean Sea	22°N	75°W	15
West Siberian Plain, Asia	62°N	75°E	29
West Virginia, state in United States	39°N	81°W	41
Western Samoa, island country in Pacific Ocean	14°S	172°E	39
White Sea, Europe	65°N	37°E	28
Williston Lake, North America	56°N	124°W	26
Winnipeg, Lake, North America	53°N	98°W	27
Wisconsin, state in United States	45°N	90°W	41
Wrangel Island, Asia	71°N	180°E	29
Wyoming, state in United States	43°N	107°W	41

Y

Yablonovyy Range, Asia	53°N	115°E	29
Yamal Peninsula, Asia	70°N	70°E	28
Yangtze, river in Asia	30°N	118°E	21
Yellow Sea, Asia	35°N	124°E	21
Yemen, country in Middle East	15°N	47°E	36
Yenisey, river in Asia	65°N	86°E	29
Yugoslavia, country in Europe	44°N	20°E	31
Yukon, river in North America	64°N	139°W	26

Z

Zargreb, capital of Croatia	46°N	16°E	31
Zaysan, Lake, Asia	48°N	84°E	29
Zurich, city in Switzerland	47°N	9°E	33

Scott E. Morris is an associate professor of geography at the University of Idaho where his current areas of teaching and research interest include mountain geomorphology, field methods, and human impact on the landscape process. Dr. Morris received his Ph.D. from the University of Colorado, Boulder and is published prolifically on the formation and climatic history of mountain landscapes, the effects of wildfire and mineral resource extraction on soil erosion processes, and the influence of water diversion and channel modification on sediment transport.